Continuing Innovation
IN INFORMATION TECHNOLOGY

Workshop Report

Committee on Continuing Innovation in Information Technology

Computer Science and Telecommunications Board

Division on Engineering and Physical Sciences

The National Academies of
SCIENCES · ENGINEERING · MEDICINE

THE NATIONAL ACADEMIES PRESS
Washington, D.C.
www.nap.edu

THE NATIONAL ACADEMIES PRESS   500 Fifth Street, NW   Washington, DC 20001

This publication is based on work supported by the National Science Foundation under Grant No. IIS-1343663. Any opinions, findings, conclusions, or recommendations expressed in this publication are those of the authors and do not necessarily reflect the views of the National Science Foundation.

International Standard Book Number-13: 978-0-309-43724-0
International Standard Book Number-10: 0-309-43724-5
Digital Object Identifier: 10.17226/23393

Additional copies of this report are available for sale from the National Academies Press, 500 Fifth Street, NW, Keck 360, Washington, DC 20001; (800) 624-6242 or (202) 334-3313; http://www.nap.edu.

Copyright 2016 by the National Academy of Sciences. All rights reserved.

Printed in the United States of America

Suggested citation: National Academies of Sciences, Engineering, and Medicine. 2016. *Continuing Innovation in Information Technology: Workshop Report.* Washington, DC: The National Academies Press. doi:10.17226/23393.

Acknowledgment of Reviewers

This report has been reviewed in draft form by individuals chosen for their diverse perspectives and technical expertise, in accordance with procedures approved by the Report Review Committee. The purpose of this independent review is to provide candid and critical comments that will assist the institution in making its published report as sound as possible and to ensure that the report meets institutional standards for objectivity, evidence, and responsiveness to the study charge. The review comments and draft manuscript remain confidential to protect the integrity of the deliberative process. We wish to thank the following individuals for their review of this report:

Ben Shneiderman, University of Maryland,
Butler W. Lampson, Microsoft Research,
Kathleen Kingscott, IBM Corporation,
Robert F. Sproull, University of Massachusetts, Amherst,
Edward D. Lazowska, University of Washington, and
Mark A. Horowitz, Stanford University.

Although the reviewers listed above have provided many constructive comments and suggestions, they were not asked to endorse the conclusions or recommendations, nor did they see the final draft of the report before its release. The review of this report was overseen by Samuel H. Fuller, Analog Devices, who was responsible for making certain that an independent examination of this report was carried out in accordance with institutional procedures and that all review comments were carefully considered. Responsibility for the final content of this report rests entirely with the authoring committee and the institution.

COMMITTEE ON CONTINUING INNOVATION IN INFORMATION TECHNOLOGY

PETER LEE, Microsoft Research, *Chair*
MARK DEAN, University of Tennessee, Knoxville
EDWARD FRANK, Brilliant Lime, Inc., and Cloud Parity Inc.
YANN LeCUN, New York University
BARBARA H. LISKOV, Massachusetts Institute of Technology
ELIZABETH MYNATT, Georgia Institute of Technology

Staff

VIRGINIA BACON TALATI, Program Officer
SHENAE BRADLEY, Senior Program Assistant

JON EISENBERG, Director, Computer Science and Telecommunications Board

COMPUTER SCIENCE AND TELECOMMUNICATIONS BOARD

FARNAM JAHANIAN, Carnegie Mellon University, *Chair*
LUIZ ANDRE BARROSO, Google, Inc.
STEVEN M. BELLOVIN, Columbia University
ROBERT F. BRAMMER, Brammer Technology, LLC
EDWARD FRANK, Brilliant Cloud, Inc., and Lime Parity, Inc.
SEYMOUR E. GOODMAN, Georgia Institute of Technology
LAURA HAAS, IBM Corporation
MARK HOROWITZ, Stanford University
MICHAEL KEARNS, University of Pennsylvania
ROBERT KRAUT, Carnegie Mellon University
SUSAN LANDAU, Google, Inc.
PETER LEE, Microsoft Corporation
DAVID E. LIDDLE, US Venture Partners
FRED B. SCHNEIDER, Cornell University
ROBERT F. SPROULL, University of Massachusetts, Amherst
JOHN STANKOVIC, University of Virginia
JOHN A. SWAINSON, Dell, Inc.
ERNEST J. WILSON, University of Southern California
KATHERINE YELICK, University of California, Berkeley

Staff

JON EISENBERG, Director
LYNETTE I. MILLETT, Associate Director

VIRGINIA BACON TALATI, Program Officer
SHENAE BRADLEY, Senior Program Assistant
EMILY GRUMBLING, Program Officer
RENEE HAWKINS, Financial and Administrative Manager

For more information on CSTB, see its website at http://www.cstb.org, write to CSTB, National Academies of Sciences, Engineering, and Medicine, 500 Fifth Street, NW, Washington, DC 20001, call (202) 334-2605, or e-mail the CSTB at cstb@nas.edu.

Preface

The 2012 National Research Council report *Continuing Innovation in Information Technology,* produced by the Computer Science and Telecommunications Board (CSTB), illustrates how fundamental research in information technology (IT), conducted at industry and universities, has led to the introduction of entirely new product categories that ultimately became billion-dollar industries. It uses examples to depict the rich interplay between academic research, industry research, and products and indicates the cross-fertilization resulting from multidirectional flows of ideas, technologies, and people. It uses a graphic (reproduced with a correction in the introduction to this report) to portray and connect areas of major investment in basic research, university-based (and largely federally funded) research, and industry research and development; the introduction of important commercial products resulting from this research; billion-dollar-plus industries (by annual revenue) stemming from it; and present-day IT market segments and representative U.S. firms whose creation was stimulated by the decades-long research. The graphic, which is of necessity incomplete and symbolic in nature, provides a framework within which additional contributions and connections can be documented and illustrated.

At a CSTB-hosted workshop on March 5, 2015, leading academic and industry researchers and industrial technologists described key research and development results and their contributions and connections to new IT products and industries, and illustrated these developments as overlays to the 2012 "tire tracks" graphic (see Box P.1 for the statement of task). The principal goal of the workshop was to collect and make available to policy makers and members of the IT community first-person narratives that illustrate the link between government investments in academic and industry research to the ultimate creation of new IT industries. Although the original plan was to have speakers also prepare papers, it proved more effective to prepare summaries of the workshop presentations based on a transcript of the proceedings and give the speakers an opportunity to review the summaries for accuracy and completeness.

This report provides summaries of the workshop presentations organized into five broad themes—(1) fueling the innovation pipeline, (2) building a connected world, (3) advancing the hardware foundation, (4) developing smart machines, and (5) people and computers—and ends with a summary of remarks from the concluding panel discussion. The narratives provide only a limited sample of the IT research ecosystem and cannot capture the full range of challenges, failures, or successes that are inherent to any research field. They do, however, provide compelling illustrations of how academic and industry research has underpinned innovation in IT and has had significant economic and other societal impacts.

Peter Lee, *Chair*
Committee on Continuing Innovation in Information Technology

BOX P.1 Statement of Task

An ad hoc committee will plan and conduct a public workshop that would highlight additional examples of the impacts of computing research using the framework established in the "tire tracks" figure published in CSTB's 2012 report *Continuing Innovation in Information Technology* and explore further uses of the figure and framework. The committee will develop the agenda for the workshop, select and invite speakers and discussants, and moderate the discussions. Invited technical leaders and researchers (primarily from industry) would use the framework to make presentations describing how academic and industry research has underpinned innovation in information technology with significant economic or other societal impact. Workshop participants would engage in discussions that build on these presentations to consider how the framework can be used to collect, display, and analyze what is known about the interplay between academic and industry research; the multidirectional flows of ideas, technologies, and people; and the impacts of research. A summary report will be prepared of the presentations and discussions at the workshop.

Contents

INTRODUCTION   1

1   **FUELING THE INNOVATION PIPELINE**   7

Application-Engaged Research for Computer Science   8
- Grounding Your Work   8
- Taking Turns   9
- Government Funding and the Amplification of Good Ideas   9

Motivators and Outcomes for Government, Academia, and Industry   10
- A Brief History of Innovation in Technology   10
- Course Corrections and Unexpected Turns   11
- The Implications of Motivations   11
- Government Funding for Industry?   13

Retaining the Leading Edge   14
- The Need for Research to Match Our Aspirations   15
- The Unpredictability Paradox   17
- Building Bridges Between Academia and Industry   18

2   **BUILDING A CONNECTED WORLD**   20

Evolving the Internet   20
- In the Beginning: The Story of ARPANET   21
- The Internet Takes Shape   22
- The Internet Reaches Out   23
- Developing the World Wide Web   24
- Lessons Learned   25

The Internet of Everything   25
- The Evolution of Enabling Technologies   26
- A Tipping Point   27

The Wireless Future   28
- Confronting Our Bandwidth Shortage   29
- The Need to Rethink Network Design   30
- Toward a Seamless Network Experience   31
- The Path from Research to Innovation   32

3   **ADVANCING THE HARDWARE FOUNDATION**   33

Developing Disruptive Architectures   34
- Hitting Inevitable Limits   34
- A History of Innovation from the Niche to the Mainstream   35
- A Disruptive Moment   36

The Winding Path of Wearables   37
Why Wearables?   37
From Fiction to Fact   38

4 DEVELOPING SMART MACHINES   41

Making Machines Learn   42
How to School a Computer   42
Tapping Big Data   43
Creating the Multilingual Computer   44
Harnessing the Wisdom of Crowds   45

Achievements in Artificial Intelligence   46
Creating the Theoretical Foundation   46
Impacts and Achievements of Research on Intelligent Machines   48
Promising Prospects for the Future   49

Robotics: From Vision to Reality   50
SLAM Dunk   50
Learning from Nature   51
Cultivating a Softer Side   52

5 PEOPLE AND COMPUTERS   54

Seeking Cybersecurity   55
Security in Transportation   56
Fighting Spam and Piracy   57

The User-Centered Design Renaissance   59
Building Toward a Sea Change   60
A New Way of Creating Technology   61

Harnessing Big Data for Social Insights   62
From Social Science to Social Media (and Back Again)   63
A New Way to Do Research   63
A Prolific Data Ecosystem   66

6 WRAP-UP DISCUSSION   67

APPENDIXES

A   **Committee Biographies**   73
B   **Presentations**   78
C   **Presenter Biographies**   80

Introduction

The past 50 years have brought tremendous advances in information technology (IT). Rapid improvements in hardware, software, and networking capabilities have transformed our everyday lives and enabled extraordinary scientific discoveries and engineering achievements. People today are virtually surrounded by information, thanks to the myriad technologies they have developed to capture, store, process, and share it. From the inner workings of the human brain to the complex mechanics of the global economy, IT is crucial to revealing how the world works and to developing data-powered innovations to improve people's lives.

The evolution from room-sized punched card computers to today's ubiquitous mobile devices, social networks, and ever-flowing streams of big data—all in an exceedingly short period of human history—is remarkable. Yet these developments were not a foregone conclusion. Few of the technologies now taken for granted could have been imagined at their beginning. Even for keen observers and visionaries, it is rarely obvious how incremental improvements, or even significant technological leaps, will spark radically new applications across diverse fields and industries. It is thus only in hindsight that the true value of precursor technologies becomes apparent. Take for example, two major technological breakthroughs that occurred in 1969: man walked on the moon, and a group of computer scientists used a new approach called packet switching to send the first message from one computer to another, a step that paved the way for the development of the Internet. Although hundreds of millions of people breathlessly watched the moon landing on live television, it is only in hindsight that it can be appreciated how profoundly packet switching would come to affect the day-to-day lives of future generations.

It is clear that technology profoundly matters in today's economy and society. IT underpins economic prosperity and national security and accelerates the pace of scientific discovery across all fields. The Internet has been shown to directly support 21 percent of gross domestic product (GDP) growth in mature economies.[1] The value that information and communication technologies bring to the U.S. GDP grew by nearly 10 percent between 2008-2013, and this sector represented 5.7 percent of the U.S. GDP in 2013.[2] With federal funding in fiscal year 2010 of less than 0.03 percent of U.S. GDP for networking and information technology research and development, this area brings a substantial return on investment for government funding.[3] Jobs in software development are projected to grow 17 percent from 2014 to 2024 to keep up with industry demand.[4]

What propelled past technological developments, and how can that momentum continue to be built on? What lessons can be gleaned from past successes—and from failures? How can technological creativity and know-how be channeled across government, academia, and the business sector to support a more prosperous, healthy, and secure future? These are some of the questions the National Academies of Sciences, Engineering, and Medicine[5] has tackled in a series of workshops and consensus studies over the past 20 years.

The 1995 National Research Council (NRC) report *Evolving the High Performance Computing and Communications Initiative to Support the Nation's Information Infrastructure,* by the Computer Science and Telecommunications Board (CSTB), offered an overview of the development of high-performance computing and communications technologies along with 13 recommendations for supporting these technologies.[6] A notable figure included in that report, often called the "tire tracks" diagram because of its resemblance to such markings, garnered significant attention in the halls of Congress, among the leadership of federal agencies, and across the research and innovation policy community. The figure, which has subsequently been updated several times, illustrates the degree to which the IT industry builds on government-funded university research, often over incubation periods of years or decades.

A few years after that seminal report, the 1999 NRC report *Funding a Revolution: Government Support for Computing Research* reviewed key advances fueled by government-supported research and articulated the economic rationale for government funding in this

---

[1]J. Manyika and C. Roxburgh, 2011, *The Great Transformer: The Impact of the Internet on Economic Growth and Prosperity,* McKinsey Global Institute, http://www.mckinsey.com/industries/high-tech/our-insights/the-great-transformer.

[2]U.S. Department of Commerce, Bureau of Economic Analysis, "Interactive Access to Industry Economic Accounts Data: GDP by Industry," release date April 21, 2016, http://www.bea.gov/iTable/iTable.cfm?ReqID=51&step=1#reqid=51&step=51&isuri=1&5114=a&5102=15 [path from www.bea.gov: Interactive Data/GDP-by-industry/Begin using the data/Gross Output by Industry/Gross Output by Industry (A) (Q)/Annual/Next Step].

[3]Networking and Information Technology Research and Development, 2009, *FY2010 Supplement to the President's Budget,* May, http://www.nitrd.gov/pubs/2010supplement/FY10Supp-FINALFormat-Web.pdf.

[4]U.S. Department of Labor, Bureau of Labor Statistics, 2016, *Occupational Outlook Handbook, 2016-17 Edition: Software Developers,* http://www.bls.gov/ooh/computer-and-informationtechnology/software-developers.htm.

[5]Effective July 1, 2015, the institution is called the National Academies of Sciences, Engineering, and Medicine. References in this report to the National Research Council are used in an historical context identifying programs prior to July 1.

[6]National Research Council (NRC), 1995, *Evolving the High Performance Computing and Communications Initiative to Support the Nation's Information Infrastructure,* National Academy Press, Washington, D.C.

area.[7] The 2003 report *Innovation in Information Technology* explored how decisions about fundamental computer science research affect progress in information technology and expanded upon the tire tracks diagram.[8] The 2009 report *Assessing the Impacts of Changes in the Information R&D Ecosystem: Retaining Leadership in an Increasingly Global Environment* examined the erosion of the U.S. leadership role in the IT sector.[9] It contains a summary of key lessons from the 2003 report, reproduced here in Box I.1.

Most recently, the 2012 NRC report *Continuing Innovation in Information Technology* described the growing size and importance of the IT sector and offered the most recent update of the tire tracks diagram[10] (reproduced, with a correction,[11] in Figure I.1).The diagram illustrates how fundamental research in IT, conducted in industry and universities, has led to the introduction of entirely new product categories that ultimately became billion-dollar industries. It uses examples to depict the rich interplay between academic research, industry research, and products and to indicate the cross-fertilization resulting from multidirectional flows of ideas, technologies, and people. Each arrow linking tracks in the figure represents a documented flow of technology within or across areas. It uses a graphic to portray and connect areas of major investment in basic research, largely at universities and largely federally funded, and industry R&D. It also shows the introduction of significant commercial products resulting from this research, billion-dollar-plus industries (by annual revenue) stemming from this research, and present-day IT market segments and representative U.S. firms whose creation was stimulated by the decades-long research. The graphic, which is of necessity incomplete and symbolic in nature, provides a framework within which additional contributions and connections can be documented and illustrated.

A common thread running through these past Academies reports has been a core finding that many of the technological breakthroughs and impacts seen over the past decades have resulted from a innovation ecosystem at the intersection of the federal government, academic research, industry research and development, and product development. These reports demonstrate how the government–academia–industry IT innovation ecosystem works, why it works, and what the future prospects for such research could

---

[7]NRC, 1999, *Funding a Revolution: Government Support for Computing Research,* National Academy Press, Washington, D.C.

[8]NRC, 2003, *Innovation in Information Technology,* The National Academies Press, Washington, D.C.

[9]NRC, 2009, *Assessing the Impacts of Changes in the Information R&D Ecosystem: Retaining Leadership in an Increasingly Global Environment,* The National Academies Press, Washington, D.C.

[10]NRC, 2012, *Continuing Innovation in Information Technology,* The National Academies Press, Washington, D.C.

[11]The computer architecture to microprocessors track in Figure 1.1 has been corrected from the 2012 version. The computer architecture to microprocessor track in the 2012 version of the figure had its origins in the reduced instruction set computing (RISC) track in the 1995 figure. However, given that the current track is labeled in terms of computer architecture and microprocessors more generally, it is more accurate to (1) adjust the academic and industry research tracks to start in 1965 because architecture research predates microprocessors and indeed goes back to the origin of computing in the 1940s and (2) reflect the market size for microprocessors more generally by starting the product track in 1971 (when Intel released the 4004), and making the line solid at 1981, when the microprocessor industry reached $1 billion in revenue.

Introduction

BOX I.1 Lessons About the Nature of Research in Information Technology—A Summary

THE RESULTS OF RESEARCH

—America's international leadership in IT—leadership that is vital to the nation—springs from a deep tradition of research. . . .

—The unanticipated results of research are often as important as the anticipated results—for example, electronic mail and instant messaging were by-products of research in the 1960s that was aimed at making it possible to share expensive computing resources among multiple simultaneous interactive users. . . .

—The interaction of research ideas multiplies their impact—for example, concurrent research programs targeted at integrated circuit design, computer graphics, networking, and workstation-based computing strongly reinforced and amplified each another. . . .

RESEARCH AS A PARTNERSHIP

—The success of the IT research enterprise reflects the complex relationship between government, industry, and universities. . . .

—The federal government has had and will continue to play an essential role in sponsoring fundamental research in IT—largely university-based—because it does what industry does not and cannot do. . . . Industrial and governmental investments in research reflect different motivations, resulting in differences in style, focus, and time horizon. . . .

—Companies have little incentive to invest significantly in activities whose benefits will spread quickly to their rivals. . . . Fundamental research often falls into this category. By contrast, the vast majority of corporate research and development (R&D) addresses product and process development. . . .

—Government funding for research has leveraged the effective decision making of visionary program managers and program office directors from the research community, empowering them to take risks in designing programs and selecting grantees. . . . Government sponsorship of research, especially in universities, also helps to develop the IT talent used by industry, universities, and other parts of the economy. . . .

THE ECONOMIC PAYOFF OF RESEARCH

—Past returns on federal investments in IT research have been extraordinary for both U.S. society and the U.S. economy. . . . The transformative effects of IT grow as innovations build on one another and as user know-how compounds. Priming that pump for tomorrow is today's challenge.

—When companies create products using the ideas and workforce that result from federally sponsored research, they repay the nation in jobs, tax revenues, productivity increases, and world leadership. . . .

SOURCE: Reprinted from National Research Council, 2009, *Assessing the Impacts of Changes in the Information Technology R&D Ecosystem*, The National Academies Press, Washington, D.C., p. 33, summarizing National Research Council, 2003, *Innovation in Information Technology*, The National Academies Press, Washington, D.C., pp. 2-4.

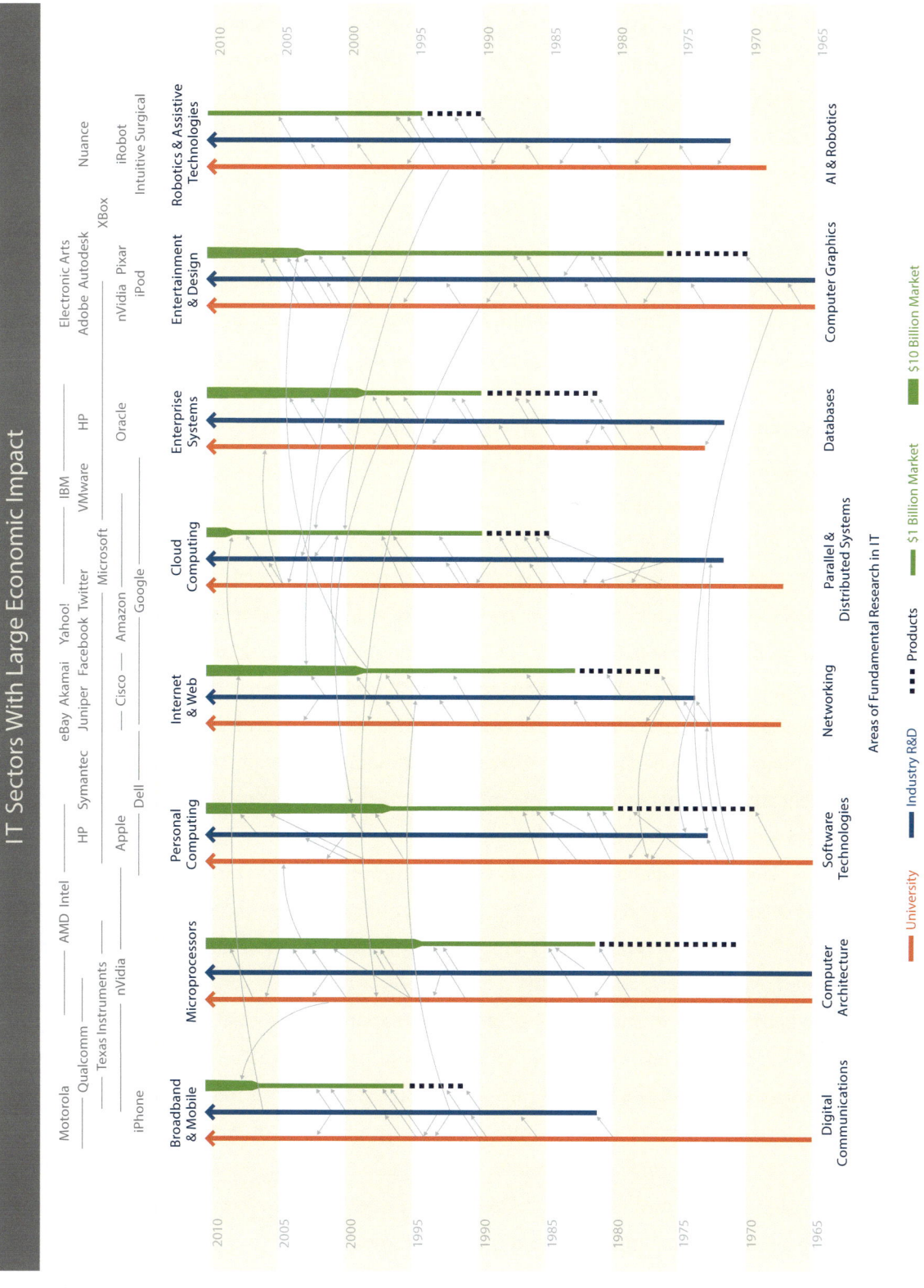

FIGURE I.1 Examples of the contributions of federally supported fundamental research to the creation of IT sectors, firms, and products with large economic impact. SOURCE: Reprinted from National Research Council, 2012, *Continuing Innovation in Information Technology*, The National Academies Press, Washington, D.C.

be, depending on how—and how much—the nation invests in it.

It is from this context that the impetus for the Continuing Innovation in Information Technology workshop emerged. With support from the National Science Foundation (NSF), the CSTB of the National Academies of Sciences, Engineering, and Medicine convened a committee of experts to organize and host a workshop exploring how academic and industry research has underpinned innovation in information technology and has had significant economic or societal impact. Chaired by Peter Lee, corporate vice president of Microsoft Research, the workshop provided a venue for invited technical leaders and researchers, primarily representing the business sector, to exchange first-person narratives illustrating the link between government investments in academic and industry research and the ultimate creation of new information technology industries. Speakers were asked to build upon the framework of the tire tracks diagram to collect, display, and analyze what is known about the interplay between academic and industry research; the multidirectional flows of ideas, technologies, and people; and the impacts of research in this area. Held in Washington, D.C., on March 5, 2015, the workshop included 15 presenters (see Appendix C).

By collecting and comparing narratives from multiple IT fields and applications, this report offers a window into how government funding has directly and indirectly led to innovations that have yielded—or are poised to yield—huge economic gains nationally and globally. Speakers traced the roles of funding and leadership from government bodies such as NSF, the Defense Advanced Research Projects Agency, the National Aeronautics and Space Administration, the Office of Naval Research, and the U.S. Congress in enabling progress across a wide range of technologies and applications, including mobile applications, wearable technology, robotics, artificial intelligence, wireless technology, cybersecurity, and numerous other areas.

Underlying many of these stories is a common theme that government funding and academic research not only have made considerable past contributions to the knowledge foundation on which the IT industry is built, but also have played a unique and essentially irreplaceable role in the development of groundbreaking new technologies. While the structures and incentives of the business sector are ideal for incrementally improving products and capitalizing on new technologies to create valuable products and services, government and academia are best suited to advance transformative research. It is through the combination of and interchange among all of these sectors that we can reap the biggest gains. IT has yielded uncountable economic, scientific, and quality-of-life benefits over the past decades. Understanding how the innovation ecosystem works is critical to keeping it going in the decades to come.

1

Fueling the Innovation Pipeline

Ask someone to draw a picture of an innovator and you're likely to get some version of Thomas Edison or Benjamin Franklin—a prolific lone genius fueled by astounding creativity and an almost magical ability to intuit what the world needs. In truth, however, innovation is not so much a person as a process—and a rather meandering, messy, and long process at that.

Take a close look at any single information technology (IT) advance and you're bound to find behind it a sprawling network of inventors, researchers, engineers, investors, and precursor technologies. Though it certainly has its heroes, innovation in information technology is the story of collaboration, borrowing, and exchange among many, many contributors over the course of years and decades.

Neither the private sector, nor university researchers, nor the federal government has a monopoly on IT innovation. It is the interplay among these contributors, with their disparate motivations, strengths, and limitations, that creates the innovation ecosystem in which theories and ideas can lead to the experimentation that spawns technologies and, ultimately, applications.

In this chapter, three leading innovators dissect the research-to-application pipeline from different perspectives: Deborah Estrin on the value of application-engaged research; Robert Colwell on the motivations of different stakeholders within the IT innovation ecosystem; and Farnam Jahanian, on the sometimes unpredictable journey from insight to innovation—and the imperative for the United States to remain at the forefront of IT.

APPLICATION-ENGAGED RESEARCH FOR COMPUTER SCIENCE

In the medical community, the process of translating findings from fundamental research into practical applications is known as translational research. It's a process that can take 10-20 years as basic chemistry or biology research is applied to develop new drugs, medical devices, or other innovations that improve medical care. The analogous process in computer science is sometimes called "application-engaged research," and in this field the invention-to-innovation cycle can happen far more quickly. This rapid cycle is a significant driver behind the enormous growth in the technology sector.

A presentation by Deborah Estrin, professor of computer science at Cornell Tech and professor of public health at Weill Cornell Medical College, focused on this critical relationship between the invention of a new tool or technique and the innovation that happens through its use. It was a theme echoed throughout much of the workshop, from Rodney Brooks's exploration of the back-and-forth process of building robots to Jaime Carbonell's description of data-driven machine learning techniques.

Estrin has spent her career on application-engaged research, often at the intersection of technology and health. A pioneer in the field of networked sensing—the use of mobile and wireless technology to collect real-time data about the physical world—she currently directs the Small Data Lab at Cornell Tech. There, her team develops technologies that harness what she terms "small data," the small bits of information generated from the personal technology we use every day, for applications that support healthy living and other goals.

Grounding Your Work

Estrin has long been focused on the application-engaged research, which she calls "grounding your work." She pointed to advice she received from Jim Waldo, now chief technology officer at Harvard University, that helped crystalize the focus on the solution-oriented research that has characterized her career: Waldo called for researchers to avoid wasting time thinking of creative *problems*, and instead spend time thinking of creative *solutions* to problems that someone in the world has articulated.

Another remark of Estrin: She has always remembered Judea Pearl, professor of computer science at the University of California, Los Angeles, a 2011 Turing Award winner and a renowned researcher in the field. Pearl once commented to a Ph.D. student, "That your approach is generalizable does not release you from the responsibility of showing us one thing it actually does." To Estrin, this sums up the idea that innovation is most successful if it is grounded in actual use.

She cited government programs as having fueled much of her work. Even serving on government-led committees has had a huge impact on the application-engaged work she does today: Her tenure at the Information Science and Technology study group of the Defense Advanced Research Projects Agency (DARPA) inspired her to pursue networked sensing. She said DARPA's other programs, such as SensIT (Sensor Information Technology) and NEST (Network Embedded Systems Technology), allowed her to keep that research moving forward.

Taking Turns

The relationship between invention and innovation, or research and application, is a two-way street, not a unidirectional flow, said Estrin. She continued, "When you're doing this kind of multidisciplinary application-driven work, as Margaret [Martonosi] said a decade ago, you have to take turns." To Estrin, this means that researchers and technologists should not insist on innovating on the "how" and the "what" at the same time, but rather oscillate between the two in order to solve both theoretical and practical problems effectively. Furthermore, any line of inquiry may be rapidly and surprisingly enriched by development from another line, propelling one's own work forward.

As an example, Estrin and her team leveraged funding from the National Science Foundation (NSF) to include different domain experts in their work in order to take turns to propel co-innovation in networked sensing. While she was conducting her research into networked sensing, smartphone use rose substantially and at the same time there was a big leap forward in methods of statistical analysis. Pairing those developments with her own inventions inspired her research focus today: improving health management using mobile devices, sensors, and the digital transactions of individuals. Estrin observed that the NSF's Science and Technology Centers program has given her research group the "funding and time to really bring the domain experts into the same room and process for a long enough period of time that we could take on authentically application-driven problems that transformed both the applications and the technology."

According to her, once a product can be used, "reality gets to push back," and it is this push and pull between research and the real world that drives innovation. In her own research experience, she said, "Scientists and engineers who were trying to measure something specifically gave us concreteness; it pushed back on us to give up on some of the things that we thought were most elegant and focus on a different set of problems that turned into effective technology for them and also led us to new technical challenges."

Government Funding and the Amplification of Good Ideas

Estrin credits government funding with allowing her to take on a wider range of problems than would be possible in an industry setting, with its necessary focus on near-term business models. Building, testing, and using working systems requires patience and committed funding. The interplay between invention and innovation also tends to amplify good ideas and make it clear what the nonuseful ideas are. Shared and open-source tools, she said, represent one good idea with roots in government-funded research that was amplified through this push and pull. The Internet protocol suite, Web browsers, and TinyOS are other examples of powerful open-source tools that industry would not or could not have invented without government-supported work.

As was pointed out by several participants, a key difference between university research and industry research is the former is not constrained by specific business models and the financial market's pressure for annual revenue targets. "It's so important that this work also happen in the university, because the university can take on problems that extend beyond the incentive structure of any individual product, company, or industry," said Estrin. Health care, she said, is a particularly clear example of a field in which university research, especially in health care IT, has propelled research that the private sector was not willing to do. With government funding, academic researchers have taken on, and can continue to take on, a broader range of problems in application-engaged work that moves technology forward for health care and many other fields.

MOTIVATORS AND OUTCOMES FOR GOVERNMENT, ACADEMIA, AND INDUSTRY

As someone with a long history working at the forefront of the technology industry, Robert Colwell offered a unique perspective on the processes and motivators behind technology research and development in government, academia, and industry. He spent most of his career engineering microprocessors at Intel, where he was chief architect on the Pentium Pro, Pentium II, Pentium III, and Pentium 4 microprocessors. After retiring from Intel, he served as director of DARPA's Microsystems Technology Office.

Although Colwell has not himself been the recipient of federal grants for academic research since his graduate studies, he is a strong believer in the inherent value of such investments. In addition, Colwell emphasized in his presentation the importance of military technology as a driver of technological advances in the commercial sector. As technology developed for military applications is adopted for public and commercial use, government investments in computer science and engineering pay double dividends.

A Brief History of Innovation in Technology

Colwell presented a brief history of technological innovation, beginning with an example of one of the earliest known computers: In 1943, John Mauchly and J. Presper Eckert built a machine for the U.S. military that quickly computed the math and physics relevant to the angles at which ballistic shells drop and explode. By the 1960s, computers were enormous but fast, becoming a part of mainstream research. At the same time, the military continued investing in improving computing capabilities to tackle more complex military problems. In the 1970s, the first microprocessors were invented, allowing computers to get substantially smaller. The 1980s brought faster microprocessors and the invention of the personal computer. In the 1990s, computers continued to improve, and the Internet and cell phones emerged. The 2000s brought smartphones and tablets, the rise of search engines, an explosion in social media, and hundreds of other innovations now prevalent in the daily life of billions of people.

Course Corrections and Unexpected Turns

Colwell stressed that one main lesson to be drawn from the history of technology in the modern era is that it is impossible to predict how government-funded technology will be adapted and used. A story from Intel illustrates the unexpected turns innovation can take: When Colwell began working on a computer chip in 1990, the Internet wasn't yet a pervasive aspect of personal computing, so the engineers did not factor it into the chip's capabilities. By 1995 when the chip was finally ready, the Internet had evolved, and it was partly a matter of luck that the chip did not need severe redesign to accommodate that new market. Even at the frontlines of the technology industry, the Internet came as a surprise. "Fundamentally, even for people in the industry designing the actual hardware, we didn't know what was coming next," he said.

Researchers have never been able to accurately predict what faster, stronger, better computers will enable. But, while one cannot predict the future, one can extrapolate from the past. And what the past tells us, according to Colwell, is that the computing technology that has transformed our world would not have been possible without government-funded academic research. Using a smartphone as an example, he listed numerous component technologies that stemmed from government-funded research, including the Internet browser, the camera, GPS, the embedded antenna, and the battery, among others (Figure 1.1). "We've never been any good at predicting what better computers will enable . . . . We just have a faith that better technology is better technology, and smart people will figure out something really cool to do with it," said Colwell.

The Implications of Motivations

While industry, academia, and government all conduct research, they have very different motivations. Based on his experience in a long industry career, Colwell attested to the reality that for-profit companies take a narrow, short-term view of technology. Whereas academic researchers might be able to step back and examine the larger picture, a company focused on earnings doesn't always have that luxury. He said that industry is also

FIGURE 1.1 Impact of direct government research on smartphones. SOURCE: Robert Colwell, "The Crucial Role of Government Funding for IT," presentation to the workshop, March 5, 2015, http://sites.nationalacademies.org/cs/groups/cstbsite/documents/webpage/cstb_160415.pdf.

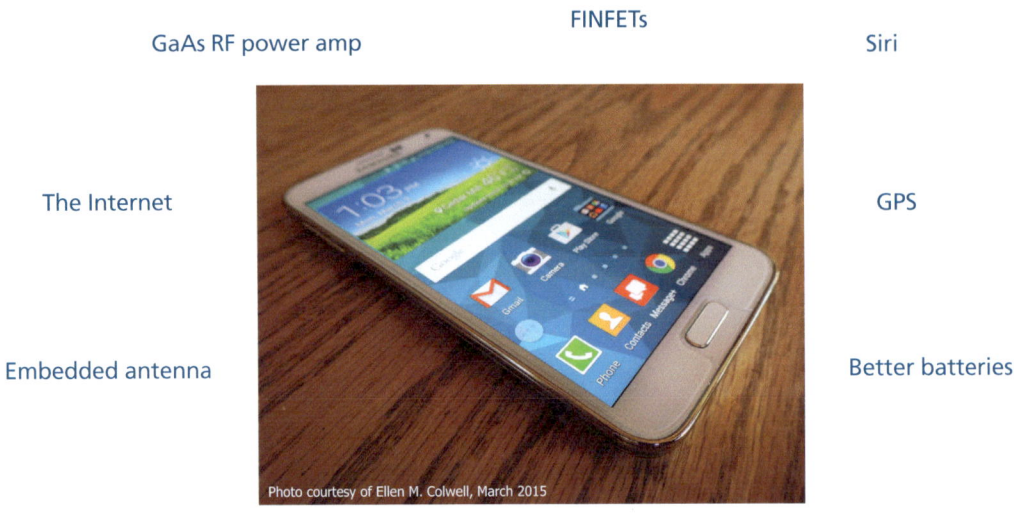

looking to sell things on a large scale. The implication of this is that if a new technology is not immediately going to sell 10 million units, it may not be worth risking money to develop it.

Of course, no one knows what product or innovation will or will not sell millions of units at some point in the future. Colwell shared that when he was at Intel, they were blind to the potential of mobile computing. Other examples of inventions we might not have without government research funding include the computer mouse, computer graphics programs, and the Internet. Government funding also supports Ph.D. students to carry out all of this research and design work. Colwell's own doctoral work in the early 1980s was sponsored by the U.S. Army.

As a demonstration of one of industry's inherent limitations, Colwell recalled that in the first years of the Internet, AOL, CompuServe, and other early e-mail and Internet providers had carved out separate online spaces that worked fine on their own, but intercommunication was complex and cumbersome. Today, in part because of government investment, we all benefit from the convenience and speed of one giant, interconnected Internet.

Turning his focus to the future, Colwell identified some current problems that he believes only academic researchers will have the motivation and perspective to solve. These include working at both the exascale and the nanoscale, improved semiconductors, and energy-efficient computing. Semiconductors present an especially worrisome challenge: Because transistors can only get so small, there will be an ultimate limit to how many circuits or transistors engineers can place on a computer chip. He warned that the time is coming when this inevitable limit will lead technological innovations to stagnate, with potentially major consequences for the U.S. economy and military. Although technology companies will certainly benefit from the research geared toward solving these problems, he urged that we cannot leave it to them, with their short-term, profit-driven view, to solve them.

Government Funding for Industry?

Although Colwell stressed that *academic* research is a main driver of unexpected innovation, he also said the government stands to gain from directly funding *industry* research. Although IT companies invest large sums in research and development, they need assurances that they will see a return on that investment. Granting government research funds directly to companies makes it more feasible for them to invest in high-risk, high-payoff innovations. Industry is competitive, not cooperative, and government funding can encourage otherwise risky development that can lead to economic growth.

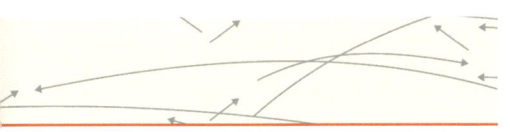

> It is virtually impossible to find any sector of our economy today that does not rely heavily on computing innovations that have come as a result of government-funded research in both academia and industry.

Another reason for government to fund industry research comes down to simple self-interest, explained Colwell. The success of the nation as a whole requires access to the best electronics. Many branches of government, but the military especially, rely heavily on commercially produced electronics. Counterfeit chips and cybersecurity concerns are very real threats. The car industry also relies heavily on industrially produced electronics. He noted that it is of great benefit to the nation as a whole if those electronics are the best and the most secure that they can be. Other important roles for the government in industry research and development, he added, include developing fair standards, creating cooperative task forces, and brokering disputes.

It is virtually impossible to find any sector of our economy today that does not rely heavily on computing innovations that have come as a result of government-funded research in both academia and industry. Today's health care, science, manufacturing, communications, and entertainment, to name just a few examples, are heavily computer-dependent. Government funding of research and development across the board increases the chances that our scientists can develop and exploit every technological opportunity and remain the world's IT leader. Colwell concluded: "We don't know what's next, but we need to win."

RETAINING THE CUTTING EDGE

With a distinguished career spanning academia, industry, and government, Farnam Jahanian, Carnegie Mellon University, has experienced the computer science discovery and innovation ecosystem from several distinct vantage points. He served as a computer science professor at the University of Michigan, as a researcher at IBM's T.J. Watson Research Center, and as assistant director of NSF for Computer and Information Science and Engineering (CISE). As leader of the CISE directorate, he was responsible for a research budget of roughly $900 million.

To frame his presentation about the role of government-funded research in technology innovation, Jahanian shared two favorite quotes about innovation:

Innovation distinguishes between a leader and a follower.
—Steve Jobs, Apple CEO and renowned innovator

The guy who invented the first wheel was an idiot.
The guy who invented the other three, he was a genius.
—Sid Caesar, comedian

Echoing a theme that pervaded the workshop, Jahanian emphasized the tremendous importance of research-driven IT to America's economy, security, and scientific leadership over the past 30 years. In his view, it is primarily IT advances that have made the U.S. economy competitive and sustainable in a global market. In addition, IT has undoubtedly accelerated the pace of scientific discovery in disciplines such as biology, chemistry, physics, and the social sciences, all of which have undergone remarkable transformations driven by computational and data-intensive approaches.

Today, Jahanian said, IT advances and interdisciplinary approaches are crucial to addressing society's most pressing challenges, including health care, cybersecurity, transportation, and environmental sustainability. Because IT is now embedded in these fields, new advances or solutions must incorporate multidisciplinary approaches that involve computer scientists and technologists, as well as domain experts. "Our community is in the middle of all of these conversations, and many of these advances will depend on involvement of members of our community and computational and data-intensive approaches," said Jahanian.

> **BOX 1.1 Top 12 Economically Disruptive Technologies (by 2025)**
>
> | | |
> |---|---|
> | Mobile Internet | Next-generation genomics |
> | Automation of knowledge work | Energy storage |
> | The Internet of Things | 3D printing |
> | Cloud technology | Advanced materials |
> | Advanced robotics | Advanced oil and gas exploration and recovery |
> | Autonomous and nearly autonomous vehicles | Renewable energy |
>
> SOURCE: J. Manyika, M. Chui, and J. Bughin, 2013, *Disruptive Technologies: Advances That Will Transform Life, Business, and the Global Economy,* McKinsey Global Institute, http://www.mckinsey.com/industries/high-tech/our-insights/the-great-transformer.

The Need for Research to Match Our Aspirations

Clearly, the United States has been a global leader in spurring the IT advances we enjoy today. A 2013 report by international business consulting firm McKinsey & Company lists 12 top "disruptive technologies," or innovations that will transform the global economy and daily lives (Box 1.1).[1] According to Jahanian, all of these technologies are rooted in basic research advances that scientists working in America have been responsible for inventing and advancing through innovations such as advanced robotics, the Internet of Things, and the mobile Internet. Furthermore, nearly all of those basic research advances have stemmed from government support. "U.S. taxpayers have long been the most important investors in knowledge creation in this country," Jahanian said.

But despite these past successes, he stressed that America's work is far from over. America today faces relentless international competition to create or capitalize on the next disruptive technologies and to recruit the best talent from around the world. Although U.S. scientists have been the recipients of the largest R&D budget for many years, other countries are beginning to understand how government-funded research leads to economic prosperity and are rapidly increasing their research spending. At China's current rate of funding growth, for example, the Chinese R&D budget is expected to surpass that of the United States by 2022.[2] Now that other countries are realizing just how critical this pipeline is, Jahanian stressed the increasing need to align U.S. R&D funding to match its scientific and economic aspirations and national security requirements.

---

[1] J. Manyika, M. Chui, and J. Bughin, 2013, *Disruptive Technologies: Advances That Will Transform Life, Business, and the Global Economy,* McKinsey Global Institute, http://www.mckinsey.com/business-functions/business-technology/our-insights/disruptive-technologies.

[2] M. Grueber and T. Studt, 2013, *2014 Global R&D Funding Forecast,* Battelle and *R&D Magazine,* December, https://www.battelle.org/docs/tpp/2014_global_rd_funding_forecast.pdf.

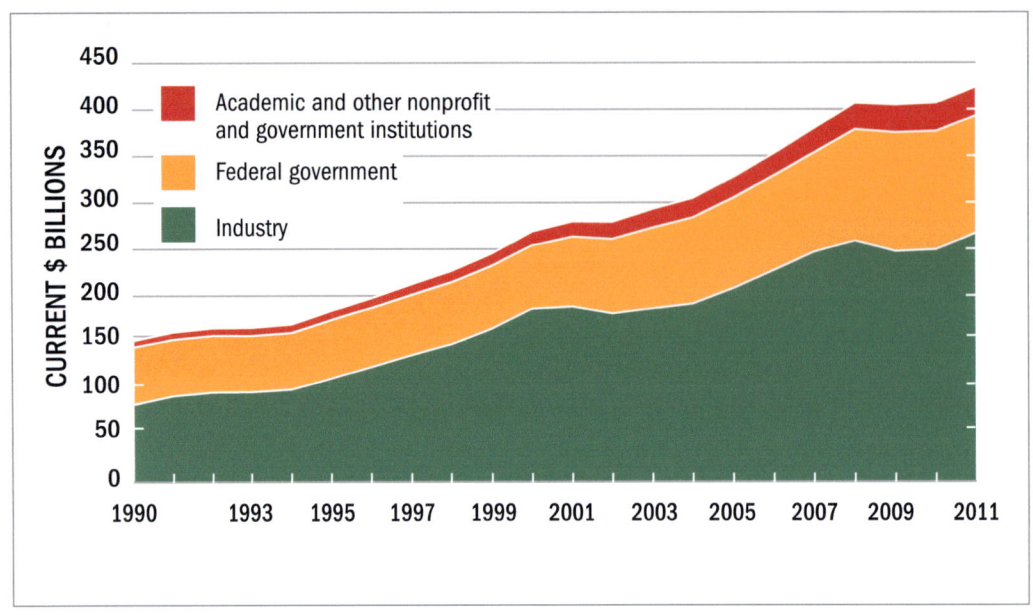

FIGURE 1.2 U.S. R&D expenditures by source of funds: 1990-2011. SOURCE: National Science Board, "National Science Board 2014 Digest: Science and Engineering Indicators," National Science Foundation, February 2014, http://www.nsf.gov/statistics/seind14/content/digest/nsb1402.pdf.

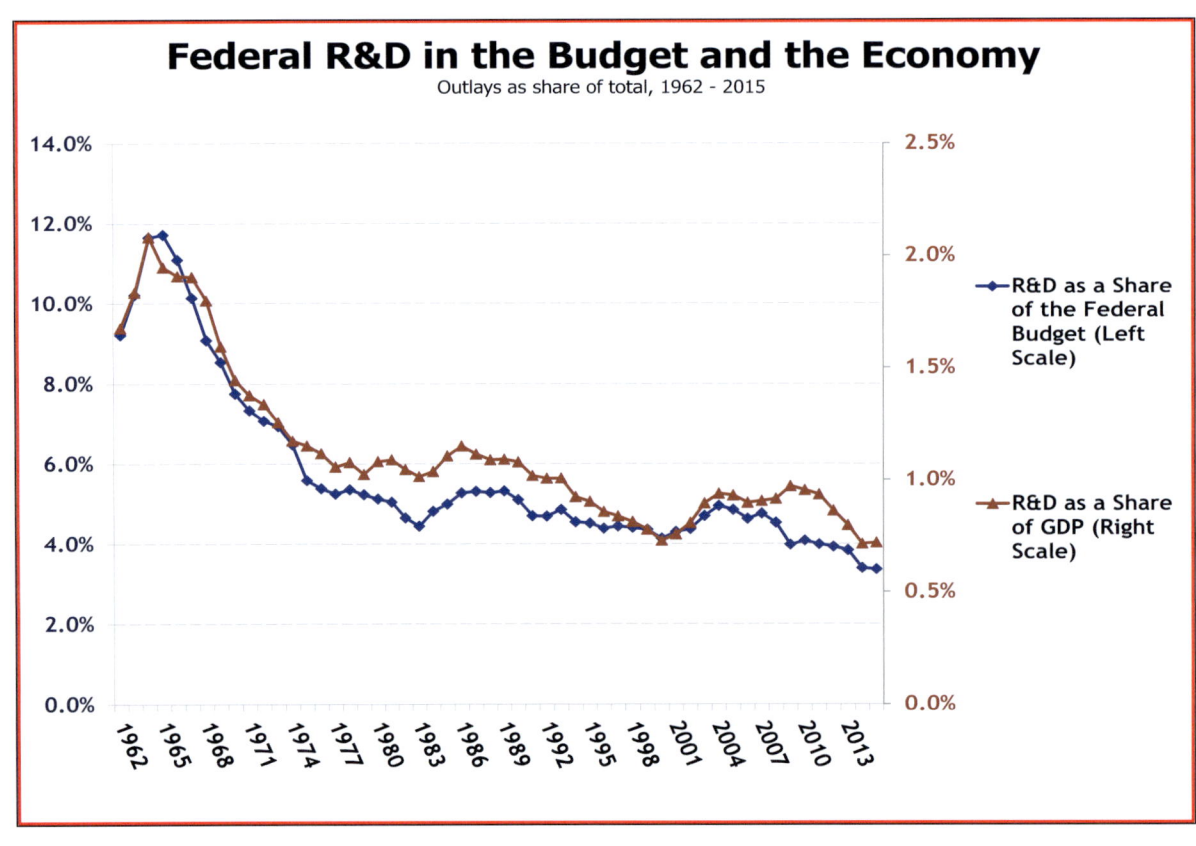

FIGURE 1.3 U.S. R&D in the budget and in the economy. SOURCE: Intersociety Working Group, *AAAS Report XXXIX: Research and Development FY 2015,* American Association for the Advancement of Science, April 2014, http://www.aaas.org/page/aaas-report-xxxix-research-and-development-fy-2015.

Two more statistics drive home this point. Right now, industry spends more money on research and development than does the U.S. government (Figure 1.2).³ This is concerning, in Jahanian's view, because industry tends to focus on short-term, applied research rather than on the long-term fundamental work that drives true innovation. Even more concerning, there has been flat or no growth in the federal research and development budget as a share of the U.S. GDP (Figure 1.3).⁴ As nearly every workshop presenter emphasized, the innovations that lead to new technologies, and thus to economic growth, come from unexpected places but have the common denominator of federal funding of basic research that is tied to meaningful problems. A growing funding gap thus threatens to undermine U.S. momentum in technological innovation.

The Unpredictability Paradox

The thriving U.S. research community drives the long-term discovery and innovation that is the foundation of our economic prosperity and domestic security. Yet the paradox when funding research projects is that their outcomes are unpredictable. There is no single path or action that leads directly from invention to innovation, from product to prosperity. "The paradox of discovery and innovation is that no one actually knows how an idea or an innovation will impact the world," said Jahanian. Sometimes an idea requires a long incubation period, during which it interacts with and reacts to other ideas and technologies before it blossoms into a groundbreaking new application. In fact, as many workshop presenters emphasized, it is most often the case that unanticipated research results are just as important or impactful as the anticipated ones. As a result, Jahanian said, "Quantifying return on investment in the context of basic research often is a very very ambiguous proposition."

The United States can take great pride in its long history of research and development. In 1945, Vannevar Bush's report on federal funding for scientific research laid a challenge the government quickly realized was worthwhile.⁵ In retrospect, there is a clear and direct path from Cold War–era federal defense contracts to today's Silicon Valley success stories. But when early federal defense contracts were awarded to develop ARPANET, a crucial precursor to today's Internet, no one could have predicted that Silicon Valley and its businesses and innovations would be a downstream result.

---

³National Science Board, 2014, *Science and Engineering Indicators: 2014 Digest,* Washington, D.C.
⁴M. Hourihan, 2015, *Federal R&D in the FY2015 Budget: An Introduction,* American Association for the Advancement of Science, Washington, D.C.
⁵V. Bush, 1945, *Science, The Endless Frontier: A Report to the President,* U.S. Government Printing Office, Washington, D.C.

Building Bridges Between Academia and Industry

The federal government is a major partner in America's discovery and innovation ecosystem, both through direct funding of research and projects and through overarching investments in nurturing the ecosystem itself. In *The Entrepreneurial State,* Mariana Mazzucato debunks the myth of a slow-moving government lagging behind frenzied innovators and reveals the opposite to be true.[6] Jahanian explained that recent national initiatives, such as the Brain Initiative, the National Robotics Initiative, and the Materials Genome Initiative, demonstrate how targeted federal investments can help solve large-scale, pressing national challenges that would be impossible for one company, university, or research organization to solve alone.

Of course, companies, universities, and research organizations are also crucial partners in the innovation ecosystem, he continued. It is where they intersect that research leads to the consumer products that drive our economy and encourage the government to reinvest in the research cycle. Historically, university research labs are where knowledge creation and information dissemination begin. Jahanian noted that in these labs, students, seed technologies, and scientific curiosity become the paths to start-ups, patents, and hardware and software prototypes that ultimately become the everyday technologies that are an integral part of our world.

Contrary to what some would assume, there is in fact a very healthy relationship between university research and industry products, and today start-ups and university labs are more connected than ever, he said. According to an annual study by the Association of University Technology Managers, there were 4,200 actively operating university start-ups in 2013, double the number in 2000.[7] This ecosystem can in part be traced to the Bayh-Dole Act, enacted in 1980, which permitted licensing agreements between university laboratories and companies, thus giving universities the ability to patent their inventions and retain the rights, creating additional incentives for them to partner with the private sector to further their innovations.

Jahanian emphasized that universities commercialize their technologies for many reasons, although the financial incentive is often exaggerated. There is far more gain to be had in developing a product that becomes a public benefit, contributes to the larger goals of a university's mission, and enhances its reputation than in making a product that is merely profitable. Government funding frees universities from the trap of a narrow-minded focus on return on investment, allowing them to pursue the risky and highly uncertain projects that are not feasible within the confines and financial influences of industry.

---

[6]M. Mazzucato, 2013, *The Entrepreneurial State: Debunking Public vs. Private Sector Myths,* Anthem Press, United Kingdom.

[7]Association of University Technology Managers, 2014, "AUTM Licensing Activity Survey: FY2013," http://www.autm.net/resources-surveys/research-reports-databases/licensing-surveys/.

This interplay among academics, government agencies, and industry has led to a gradual shift of mindset. Transferring knowledge, whether in a general form or in the form of an actual new product, is no longer strictly about protecting intellectual property. Today's researchers see the long history of this back-and-forth and recognize that this relationship is about the pipeline from knowledge dissemination to economic development, to societal benefits.

In summary, Jahanian reiterated his firm belief that to date, federal investments in basic research have returned exceptional dividends to our nation, while also providing a foundation for economic prosperity and national security. There is no reason to slow down or stop these amazing yet unpredictable results. The jobs of the future are in this discovery and innovation ecosystem, in the fields of engineering, computing, or information technology; he urged that the federal research funds of the future must be there, too.

2

Building a Connected World

In a relatively short time, the connecting of just a few computers in the early 1970s has become an Internet that billions of people can tap into anywhere, anytime. Over the past 10 years, this connectivity has exploded into an era when nearly any device can be Internet-enabled. In a framework known as the Internet of Everything, we are now connecting not only computers and people, but also our phones, wearable technology, and home devices such as lightbulbs and thermostats. As we look to the wireless future, government investment will be key to developing new technologies to redesign cellular networks, overcome limitations on bandwidth, and advance the sensor technology that will pave the way for networked sensors in the body, increased automation of cars, and other applications that cannot yet be predicted.

The government's investment in research, early implementation of networks, and collaborations with both academic institutions and industry were instrumental in bringing about what we know today as the Internet. In this chapter, Internet pioneers share the stories of innovation in three key areas: Vint Cerf reflects on the emergence of the Internet; David Culler describes the integration of the Internet into the objects that surround us; and Andrea Goldsmith shares her perspective on the past and future of wireless technologies.

EVOLVING THE INTERNET

Vint Cerf, vice president and chief Internet evangelist at Google, focused his presentation on the government's central role in collaborations that led to the creation of the Internet.

Known as one of the fathers of the Internet, Cerf has had a front-row seat and played a leading role in the Internet's creation and has remained at the cutting edge of networking innovation throughout an illustrious career.

The history of the Internet is a clear demonstration of the crucial role of interplay among government, researchers, and industry in breaking new ground for IT advances and applications. "Every sector in our social and economic system has been engaged and continues to be engaged in the Internet," he said, adding that "we have managed to mutually reinforce the interest, capacities, and capabilities of many different parts of our social and economic system to keep the Internet growing and going."

In the Beginning: The Story of ARPANET

Cerf began with a history of the Internet's most direct predecessor, the ARPANET, which connected academic institutions funded by ARPA (now known as the Defense Advanced Research Projects Agency, or DARPA) to conduct artificial intelligence and computer science research. A primary impetus for its development was to allow collaborating institutions to share computing capacity and co-develop software.

An early collaboration between the Lincoln Laboratory at the Massachusetts Institute of Technology and the Systems Development Corporation led to a groundbreaking test around 1966 that demonstrated the potential for two separate computers to exchange blocks, or "packets" of information. About 2 years later, ARPA sent out a request for quotation to build packet switches, called interface message processors (IMPs), for the ARPANET. Bolt, Beranek, and Newman (BBN)—a technology company in Cambridge, Massachusetts—won the contract. As a result, BBN contributed a key industry component to ARPANET's evolution: Bob Kahn at BBN wrote Host to IMP Specification 1822, describing how to implement an interface that lets host computers connect to the IMP; this specification was subsequently made available to the academic participants in the ARPANET project. In today's Internet terminology, the IMP served as the ARPANET's "router," a system for orchestrating the exchange of packets of information between networked computers.

Nearly all of the foundational technologies underlying ARPANET were developed not by one person or organization but by an interdependent, collaborative network of academic, industry, and government experts and experimenters. The development of the host protocol, for example, which allows networked computers to recognize one another's identities and locations, was led primarily by Steve Crocker at the University of California, Los Angeles (UCLA), with early-stage involvement from the University of Utah and other institutions. In recounting this story, Cerf pointed out that the development of the ARPANET and subsequent Internet was not purely a U.S. pursuit. Several foreign visiting scientists at UCLA contributed to the early phases of host-to-host protocol development.

In addition, the development of Telnet, an important remote access protocol, resulted from collaborations involving UCLA, Stanford Research Institute (SRI), RAND, BBN, and the Massachusetts Institute of Technology (MIT). Development of the File Transfer Protocol was led by Abhay Bhushan at MIT, and the development of networked e-mail was led by BBN; both efforts involved numerous collaborators. Even ARPA was directly involved, with ARPANET director Larry Roberts writing one of the first TECO macros to parse and display e-mail message files—an example of ARPA not only funding research but also engaging in technology development itself.

The first public demonstration of ARPANET came in October 1972, about 3 years after nodes were installed at UCLA, SRI, the University of California, Santa Barbara, and the University of Utah. In 1975, ARPA handed over ARPANET operation to the Defense Communications Agency, now called the Defense Information Systems Agency (DISA). However, BBN continued to handle the key technical operation and ran the network operation center in Cambridge, Massachusetts.

> Nearly all of the foundational technologies underlying ARPANET were developed not by one person or organization but by an interdependent, collaborative network of academic, industry, and government experts and experimenters.

The Internet Takes Shape

From 1973 to 1974, the initial network design for the Internet began as a collaboration between Bob Kahn, who was then at ARPA, and Cerf, then a professor at Stanford University. Together they designed the TCP protocol (later, the TCP/IP Internet network protocols), a core set of protocols still used to communicate across the Internet.[1] Multiple academic, industry, and government players interacted frequently to develop the Internet's foundation. Cerf was appointed to the International Packet Network Working Group, spawned during the 1972 ARPANET demonstration. The research and development company Xerox PARC, located close to his lab at Stanford, sent its researchers to attend Stanford seminars on Internet design, contributing their experience with the PARC Universal Packet and Ethernet, two important communications technologies. In the mid-1970s and early 1980s, Cerf said, numerous academic and government researchers were using TCP/IP. With ARPA's encouragement, industry players, including some at IBM research, HP research, and the Digital Equipment Corporation (DEC) Systems Research Center, implemented TCP/IP in a research context. Despite having their own proprietary networking protocols, the companies' research teams were interested in and excited about a nonproprietary

---

[1] V.G. Cerf and R.E. Kahn, 1974, A protocol for packet network intercommunication, *IEEE Transactions on Communications* 22(5):637-648.

global network. Because these companies implemented TCP/IP in their operating systems, it was possible by January 1983 to ask that all the computers on the ARPANET and packet satellite and packet radio networks convert to TCP/IP, a step that would later play an important role in the commercialization of the Internet.[2]

As the Internet gained steam, the U.S. government helped to fuel its momentum with both formal and informal collaborations. Seeing the value of quick information exchange and shared computing power, the Department of Energy (DOE), NASA, the National Science Foundation (NSF), and DARPA all implemented their own networks: the DOE Energy Science Network, the NASA Science Internet, NSF's CSNET, and later NSF-NET, and at DARPA, the packet satellite net, the packet radio net, and ARPANET. These networks were aggregated to form the Internet.

"Government representatives themselves also collaborated very directly with regard to program planning and financing [of the Internet]," explained Cerf. "They formed something called the Federal Research Internet Coordinating Committee, which was mostly represented by program managers from DOE, NASA, NSF, and DARPA. Eventually that became formalized as the Federal Networking Council, which had representatives from many other parts of the U.S. government in addition to the four initial funding agencies."

The Internet Reaches Out

In the early 1980s commercial organizations began to recognize the potential profits in providing equipment to support the Internet. For example, 3COM, a spin-off from Xerox PARC, made commercial Ethernet devices and eventually software that ran TCP/IP. Proteon was spun off from MIT, Cisco Systems from Stanford University, and Bridge and SUN Microsystems from Stanford and the University of California, Berkeley.

In an important shift toward the late 1980s, companies began to move past the physical equipment and began offering Internet services. One step toward commercialization resulted from a collaboration between MCI, which was participating in the NSFNET backbone, and Bob Kahn's nonprofit organization, Corporation for National Research Initiatives The MCI commercial mail service was connected to the NSFNET backbone (with permission from the Federal Networking Council), even though commercial traffic was normally prohibited in the NSFNET appropriate use policy. Around the same time, three commercial Internet service providers emerged: UUNET, PSINET, and CERFNET. These were interconnected over a commercial Internet exchange that mirrored the federal Internet exchanges connecting networks at DOE, NASA, NSF, and DARPA.

---

[2] Reviewers of this report noted the important contribution of Berkeley Unix, an academic project that enhanced AT&T Unix in many ways, including by adding TCP/IP networking support. AT&T allowed it to be distributed widely to academia, which spread the use of TCP/IP. TCP/IP adoption was also encouraged by DARPA, through its funding of the SUN workstation, which ran Berkeley Unix.

A hearing before Tennessee senator Al Gore in September of 1986 marked an important milestone in the Internet's expansion. During this hearing, Senator Gore asked whether the supercomputer centers that NSF was funding should be interconnected with an optical fiber network; subsequently, NSF commissioned the design and the implementation of a backbone network for its National Research and Education Network Program while also providing subsidies for the creation of intermediate-level networks. In 1991, the passage of the High Performance Computing Act essentially established a broad initiative to create a national information infrastructure.

The next crucial milestone came in 1992, when the Boucher bill formally permitted commercial traffic on the NSFNET backbone. This collaboration between Congress, NSF, and the rest of the Internet community was a key step in the Internet development because it made it feasible to commercialize the service so that the general public could use it. Reflecting on this history, Cerf explained that many of the developments that led to the creation and expansion of the Internet would never have happened without the strong linkages between government-sponsored research programs at the universities and spinoffs that could commercialize the technology.

Developing the World Wide Web

The World Wide Web, a term coined by Tim Berners-Lee, represented the next major step toward the Internet we know today. The first components needed to make the World Wide Web were developed by Berners-Lee at CERN in 1991: the HTTP protocols, a client and server mechanism, and browser and HTML specifications. As the 1990s progressed, a number of browsers were developed, including Erwise, ViolaWWW, MidasWWW, tkWWW, Cello, Spyglass, Internet Explorer, and Firefox.

A defining moment came in 1993 when the NSF-funded National Center for Supercomputer Applications announced the first widely used graphical browser, MOSAIC, the result of an effort pushed forward by Mark Andreessen and Eric Bina despite not being a specifically sanctioned project. With the release of MOSAIC it became clear to users that the Internet could be more than a UNIX command line and could include imagery, formatted text, color, and—eventually—video and audio. The browser quickly gained popularity: "MOSAIC represented a massive transformation for the way the Internet was perceived," said Cerf.

Just a year later, Jim Clark and Marc Andreessen co-founded Netscape Communications, a company whose 1995 stock market launch would trigger the dot-com boom. As with previous Internet developments, this milestone reflected a mix of academic and industry contributions, but this time, with the involvement of the stock market. The dot-com boom continued unabated until April of 2000.

Lessons Learned

Cerf emphasized that none of these important early Internet developments would have been possible without the U.S. legislature funding the research agencies involved. "The lessons I take away from this in terms of the power of collaboration is that there was a very effective synergy realized between the government research agencies, which were persistent in their funding and willingness to take risk," he said. "There was no guarantee that this program or this project would actually materialize successfully."

During the Internet's collaborative development, numerous institutions were created to fill important needs, a process that lent the Internet its robustness and sustainability. "When we run into an issue that requires attention that seems to require institutionalization, the Internet community simply invents these things," said Cerf.

All the collaborators played key roles in the development and spread of the Internet. The academic community invented and explored networking technologies in a non-proprietary fashion. Industry set about to commercialize the technology, making it widely available. The stock market was equally important because it brought about the rapid expansion of this capital-intensive business. Finally, the U.S. legislature provided the funding and the very light regulation of the Internet environment that enabled it to grow.

The positive reinforcement cycles brought by these groups continue to this day. "The ball bounces between the legislative side, the academic side, and the industry side, and these cycles are all mutually reinforcing, and they continue to increase the availability of the Internet everywhere," said Cerf.

THE INTERNET OF EVERYTHING

As remarkable as the emergence of the Internet was, its early development was constrained to the realm of full-fledged computers. Developments since the early 2000s have cast aside these constraints and ushered in a new era in which practically anything can be connected to the Internet, from phones and watches to thermostats and lightbulbs. This framework in which people, data, processes, and objects are all interconnected through the Internet is known as "the Internet of Everything" (or, when referring primarily to devices, "the Internet of Things"). David Culler of the University of California, Berkeley, discussed research that is helping make possible a world of ubiquitous Internet-enabled devices.

Before delving into the technological evolutions that have enabled the Internet of Everything, Culler began with a review of key consumer products illustrating the expansion of the Internet outside the (computer) box. In the late 1990s, the handheld Palm

Pilot appeared on the market, Wi-Fi began allowing people to connect to the Internet on their laptops, and Qualcomm produced a small mobile phone. By the mid-2000s the first Apple iPhone brought the Internet to the mobile person and Nintendo's Wii video game console introduced sensing to computer games. The arrival of the "connected home," in which home appliances and accessories can be controlled from the Internet, was marked by the introduction of connected lightbulbs in late 2012 and the Nest thermostat in 2013. This trend continued, with the 2014 International Consumer Electronics Show revealing a shift away from tablets and smartphones to connected home devices and wearables.

The Evolution of Enabling Technologies

Culler then described how the technology necessary to connect devices such as home security systems, lightbulbs, and game controllers to the Internet stemmed from a mixture of academic, government, and industry research and development initiatives.

In particular, DARPA funding that started in 1978 and increased in the mid- to late 1990s helped encourage the development of some key underlying networking technologies to enable interconnected devices. DARPA's Sensor Information Technology (SensIT) program, for example, was created to develop software for networks of distributed microsensors for military purposes; the program led to ad hoc deployable microsensors and distributed computing methods to accurately extract timely information for detecting, classifying, and tracking a target from a sensor field.[3] Later, the DARPA Network Embedded Systems Technology (NEST) program arranged for Culler's group at the University of California, Berkeley, to create the building blocks for network-embedded systems. The program, launched in 2001, led to a microplatform known as TinyOS, which was scalable to extremely small devices in extremely large numbers and able to operate at extremely low power while remaining vigilant to potential stimuli.

NEST was designed so that all other contractors could use the platform and contribute to it, creating a rare nationwide open source hardware and software effort. At the end of the project, NEST demonstrated thousands of nodes with contractors in various locations. Although NEST was focused on military applications, these sensor networks quickly found use in many other applications. For example, the NSF-funded Center for Embedded Network Sensing at UCLA focused on applying sensor networks for environmental monitoring, tracking changes in habitats, and for other scientific applications.

In parallel with these developments, industry and academic researchers were pushing forward on numerous other technologies that would ultimately converge to enable a plethora of Internet-connected devices. The development of Linux, a free operating

---

[3] S. Kumar and D. Shepherd, 2001, SensIT: Sensor information technology for the warfighter, in *Proceedings of the 4th International Conference on Information Fusion, FUSION 2001,* http://bit.csc.lsu.edu/~iyengar/images/contributions/TuC11.pdf.

system that could run on any computer, was an important development in the 1990s. The 1990s also brought the development of smaller microprocessors and sensors and the proposal that a sensing and communication unit that at the time was about the size of a silver dollar could be made on a millimeter scale—approaching the size of dust.

Culler pointed to several academic projects from the late 1990s and early 2000s that further pushed the envelope. The Endeavour project at the University of California, Berkeley, for example, focused on making it more convenient for people to interact with information, devices, and other people.[4] Although open source software seeded this community, it suffered from a lack of hardware. In 2000, to address this deficiency, Intel formed a network of university-based "lablets," some of which worked on how to get a tremendous amount of computing into a constrained space.

In 2003, the emergence of IEEE 802.15.4 standard for low-rate wireless personal area networks was another milestone. This standard gave fundamental lower network layers a wireless personal area network that offered low-cost, low-speed, and low-power ubiquitous communication between devices. Several years later this standard and the new Internet Protocol version 6 (IPv6) came together into a new routing standard. Around 2005, NSF added momentum with its Networking Technology and Systems (NeTS) Program, a grant program soliciting proposals in four research areas: programmable wireless networks, networking of sensors, broadly defined networking, and future Internet design.[5] These developments have paved the way for a burst of new devices and applications.

A Tipping Point

By 2008, technology had converged to a point where many of the challenges of connecting small, diverse devices to the Internet had been addressed. Similarly, the development of "idle listening" solved the power consumption problem by allowing devices to monitor inputs only when they sense there is something to detect. Idle listening allowed the development of the IEEE 802.15.4e wireless standard, which is incorporated into event-driven devices and also underlies the energy-efficient Ethernet. These developments were complemented by innovations in information routing and volume management such as local rerouting and the Trickle algorithm, allowing networks and devices to continually adjust to changes in available networks and the density of users to avoid flooding the network.

---

[4]University of California, Berkeley, Electrical Engineering and Computer Science Department, 2014, "The Endeavour Expedition: Charting the Fluid Information Utility," last modified July 22, http://endeavour.cs.berkeley.edu.

[5]National Science Foundation, Program Solicitation, NSF 06-516 to replace NSF 05-505, In the Matter of: Furtherance of the President's Management Agenda in FY 2016 from the Directorate for Computer and Information Science and Engineering, Division of Computer & Network Systems, March 6, 2006, http://www.nsf.gov/pubs/2006/nsf06516/nsf06516.htm.

The combination of these advances led to a tipping point in small-device capabilities, and subsequent years have seen an explosion in the number and diversity of Internet-enabled devices for personal, home, business, and military use. Looking forward, Culler said, technology is entering a point where ensembles can be connected. "It's not my smart device, it's what happens when my smart device and a handful of them walk in with me to my home with its family of smart things that are also connected and are connected to various kinds of societal infrastructure, whether that be electric utilities or transportation," he said. Future developments would be focused on discovery, integration, physical mashups, and metadata, Culler concluded, although along with these developments would come new challenges in another key area: privacy.

THE WIRELESS FUTURE

The advent of wireless technologies has been crucial to our transition toward the Internet of Everything, and these technologies will undoubtedly grow more crucial as the trend continues. A presentation by Andrea Goldsmith of Stanford University examined technical challenges facing wireless networks and the key role of government-funded research in advancing solutions.

Reflecting on her 30-year career in wireless communication, Goldsmith said today is the most exciting time for this technology. In her view, a big difference between the wireless past and the wireless future lies in who—or what—is exchanging information. Whereas in the past most information exchange was initiated or mediated by people, in the future devices themselves will likely be driving much of the communication: "We're going from a world where we used to have people using wireless to communicate with each other and access information, and now we're moving into a world of device-to-device communication," said Goldsmith. "That's going to require a complete rethinking of how we build wireless systems."

Device-to-device communication will not only lead to new systems that we can imagine from today's vantage point, such as the next-generation cellular phone or Wi-Fi, but will also enable sensors in everything, even inside the body, she said. One potential application of these sensor networks is to develop smart homes and buildings that could, for example, lead to greater energy efficiency or detect when an elderly person suffers a fall and call for help. Goldsmith noted that health is another area where wireless technology is poised to make a huge impact. Cell phones are already changing the way medicine is done; for example, the technology already exists for someone in Africa to use a cell phone to take a photo of a blood sample and send it to a remote location for malaria detection. Goldsmith went on to explain that in-body sensors and networks also hold tremendous potential, though these will require completely new ways of communication, perhaps using chemicals or sensors on neurons to power devices. For example, sensors around an artificial heart might detect a problem and send a wireless signal to a device that could initiate a lifesaving intervention. Neuroscience offers other exciting opportunities: the Whole Brain Initiative, for example, is starting to decipher how neurons in the brain are connected and what the signals do. Already it is possible to inject a signal into a particular part of the brain and reduce some of the symptoms of Parkinson's disease; a better understanding of signal encoding and decoding in the brain might allow scientists to build a tiny transmitter and receiver to compensate for damage or disease.

Despite the allure of next-generation wireless technologies and the Internet of Things, however, Goldsmith described significant challenges on the horizon and the need for innovative solutions to enable the wireless future.

Confronting Our Bandwidth Shortage

One big challenge facing wireless technology is the inherent limits of the radio frequency spectrum—the medium through which all wireless signals are transmitted, along with signals from television, radio, GPS, and other data. The Federal Communications Commission (FCC) grants companies licenses to use slivers of this limited physical spectrum. Based on trends in the use of smartphones, a 2010 FCC report projected an almost 275 megahertz cellular spectrum deficit by 2014—a spectrum *deficit* that exceeded even the amount of spectrum being used at the time (225 megahertz).[6] The years 2010-2014 indeed saw exponential growth in demand for wireless data, primarily driven by video, and this growth exceeded the spectrum available in the cellular bands. However, these same years saw a growth in the availability of Wi-Fi networks, so users did not actually experience the full brunt of the cellular spectrum crunch.

While we may have weathered that storm, Goldsmith said current trends toward the Internet of Things point to a more concerning bandwidth shortage on the horizon—one that affects both the radio spectrum generally and Wi-Fi specifically. Forecasts indicate we will have on the order of 50 billion devices by 2020. Since wireless demands already exceed the spectrum available in the license band, Wi-Fi is making up for the current shortfall, but this cannot continue indefinitely. Wi-Fi also is interference limited, so when 20 billion devices are using the same unlicensed spectrum, Wi-Fi will face a major crunch as well.

While acknowledging a significant amount of hype building around the Internet of Things, Goldsmith explained that there is enough evidence of the trend's emergence and impact for it to be taken seriously when projecting future wireless demands. In the trans-

_____

[6] B. Reed, 2010, FCC projects 275 MHz 'spectrum deficit' by 2014, *Network World,* October 21, http://www.networkworld.com/article/2192490/wireless/fcc-projects-275mhz--spectrum-deficit--by-2014.html.

portation sector, there has been growth of automated highways, and semi-automated cars are already among us; the newest Tesla car, for example, can change lanes without driver input.[7] Similar trends are happening in the health care sector, where people are already using wearable sensors to track heartbeat, physical activity, and other variables. "If you just look at these two sectors as already emerging as economically viable, I think there's no question that the Internet of Things is going to be very real," Goldsmith said. For this reason, she said the prediction of 50 billion connected devices is not unreasonable, and even if it turns out to be only 10 billion or 20 billion, that is still much more than today's wireless communication infrastructure can handle.

Goldsmith said there is still an open question whether the deficit in bandwidth is a result of poorly designed systems, or because the systems have reached their physical capacity (also referred to as the Shannon limit of the physical layer, or the maximum rate at which data can be sent over a particular bandwidth with zero error).[8] Pointing out that the Shannon capacity of wireless channels is unknown and even less is understood about the Shannon limit of ad hoc and sensor networks, she said more research is needed in this very theoretical field to understand whether better network design could help to solve the bandwidth shortfall.

The Need to Rethink Network Design

A second problem lies in the design of cellular networks. Even though cellular technology is in its fourth generation, Goldsmith explained, the underlying design principles of today's cellular systems are identical to those of first-generation analog systems: It is still assumed, for example, that the system is interference-limited. However, multiple technological advances have emerged to address the problem of interference, including using multiple antennas, or MIMO, and multiuser detection, which was invented in the 1980s but only recently became implementable thanks to increases in computer processing power. Despite being no longer interference-limited, the overall design of the networking system has not changed to take advantage of these developments. In addition, there is a growing need for cellular networks to become more energy efficient: One unknown, for example, is the minimum amount of energy necessary for a network to operate when power is limited, such as during an event affecting the power grid.

As a result of these trends and needs, it is time for a complete rethinking of cellular design, said Goldsmith, adding that this effort needs to be driven by the research world. Only after researchers show that a new design can net an order-of-magnitude improve-

---

[7]In October 2015, Tesla Motors announced that its new software release would incorporate additional self-driving technology (Tesla Motors, "Your Autopilot Has Arrived," October 14, https://www.teslamotors.com/blog).

[8]C.E. Shannon, 1948, A mathematical theory of communication, *The Bell System Technical Journal* 27:379-423, 623-656.

ment in a cellular system will it be adopted by industry. Because of industry's focus on short-term revenue, companies cannot afford to spend the time and money on research and development to completely rethink cellular system design.

Goldsmith said that this effort will in part involve determining the most important aspects of the cellular network: Is capacity the primary concern? Or power consumption? For example, if someone is trying to connect a device powered from an energy-harvesting battery, speed may not matter as much as connecting to the cellular network with minimum energy. Coverage is another issue: Can we build a cellular system that gets coverage everywhere, including indoors?

Goldsmith pointed to millimeter wave MIMO technology as a possible solution. There is a great deal of unregulated open spectrum at 60 gigahertz or higher. However, operating at these frequencies comes with challenges. Antenna arrays containing hundreds of elements can compensate for the high attenuation, but this approach will require a new design approach. "In my view, and we're doing some research on this, we really need a complete rethinking of system design to take advantage of these technologies," she said.

Toward a Seamless Network Experience

Another challenge is how to use Bluetooth, Wi-Fi, cellular, and even other networks in a seamless way. "What I really want is a big wireless cloud," Goldsmith said. "I don't care what network I'm on, I don't need the icon on my phone telling me what wireless network I'm on, I just want it to work for whatever application I'm using."

In wired networks, a big wave of research has focused on software-defined networking, an approach that might be usable for wireless networks too. However, wireless networks are fragmented, so switching from cellular to Wi-Fi typically requires closing a session on one network and opening another. Goldsmith envisions a potential software-defined networking design for wireless devices that uses a unified control plane to match the wireless network to the application being used. For example, a low-data-rate, low-energy application might use millimeter wave, Bluetooth, or lower power Wi-Fi instead of cellular.

Energy is the driving constraint for sensor networks, explained Goldsmith. Some sensors harvest energy from the environment while others are powered by batteries. Some battery-powered sensors, such as those embedded in a structure like a bridge, must last decades without recharging. To build communication systems that use extremely low amounts of energy, Goldsmith said, we need to start from scratch. Modulation, coding, and multiple antenna techniques are all power hungry, not only in terms of transmitting energy but also in the processing power. For short-range networks, it is important to examine how much energy the circuitry consumes. Zigbee and Bluetooth may be a lot better than Wi-Fi or cellular, but it is not known if they are anywhere close to the minimum energy consumption possible, said Goldsmith, pointing to the need for more research in this area.

The Path from Research to Innovation

To conclude, Goldsmith discussed how theoretical research translates into practice and how practice can also circle back and inform research. As a case in point, Goldsmith shared the story of her first start-up, Quantenna, which she launched after about 20 years as a researcher. At the heart of this effort was her desire to build something—a desire she traced back to her first job building an antenna array in the mid-1980s, an experience she said made her fall in love with wireless communication and inspired her research career. Quantenna makes Wi-Fi chips with the goal of achieving the best performance on the market, based on Goldsmith's research in communications theory, and the company recently announced a 10 gigabytes per second Wi-Fi system that uses the most sophisticated physical layer in existence. Goldsmith cites this achievement as an example of applying deep theoretical research to build better systems. At the start-up, she said she learned that many aspects of wireless systems are poorly understood and that actually building a system revealed many questions that later fed back into her research and teaching.

She concluded her talk by pointing out that much research is still needed to realize a wireless vision, but that doing this work will allow wireless technology to change people's lives worldwide. She also said that although she thinks that research has a profound impact on technology development and vice versa, a stronger connection or feedback loop from industry to universities would offer more synergy and allow researchers in universities to solve even more important problems—and government has an important role in making this happen. "Government and government-funded research were key for the development of wireless technologies. These technologies are central to the growth and success of mobile devices, but there is still more that needs to be done to get us where we want to go," she said.

3

Advancing the Hardware Foundation

While it is software that comes to mind most readily when we think about using computers—the interfaces that we interact with, the applications we use to perform tasks—hardware is the foundation that makes all computing and communications technology possible. Behind Instagram is a camera; behind your favorite mapping app is a Global Positioning System (GPS) satellite; powering your laptop is a lithium-ion battery; central to your smartphone is its liquid crystal display (LCD) touchscreen display. As this handful of examples make clear, there are a tremendous number of component technologies making up the devices we depend on every day. In a vast majority of cases these technologies are rooted in pioneering research conducted or funded by the federal government, which later fed into other research and commercial endeavors.

Current trends suggest a future populated with ever more computing and communications technologies, from self-driving cars to gadgets that are worn on or even embedded inside the body. As we move toward this future we will continue to depend on fundamental research to overcome the limitations of current technologies and usher forth new hardware and computer architectures. This chapter summarizes presentations by Margaret Martonosi, on the evolution of computer architectures that balance capabilities and speed against the limitations of energy and heat, and Thad Starner, on the history and development of wearable computers.

DEVELOPING DISRUPTIVE ARCHITECTURES

As our computers and communication tools evolve, each new device must strike the right balance between capabilities, speed, power, and thermal constraints in order to achieve a higher level of functionality and speed without overheating or draining power too quickly. Exchange between researchers and industry has been crucial to the development of new, disruptive architectures that can overcome previous constraints and enable radically new products.

Margaret Martonosi, a professor of computer science at Princeton University, is known for her work on computer architecture. Coined in a 1964 IBM paper,[1] the term computer architecture refers to the field of computer design concerned with balancing competing factors such as computing performance, power needs, cost, and reliability. In particular, Martonosi's research has focused on power efficiency.

Martonosi described computer architecture as a mediator between computer technology—the technical challenges of building computers—and computing applications—what you can do with those computers once they are built. Today's technology landscape brings challenges and opportunities in both realms. "Since it's a very dynamic time for both the application side and the technology side, that makes it a particularly interesting time to be a computer architect," said Martonosi.

Hitting Inevitable Limits

Current computing applications are dramatically widening the scope of what computers can do. Today's computers work with a lot of data highly distributed across a diversity of devices and are much more communication-intensive than computers in the past. At the same time, new applications and functionalities are demanding more performance for computations, storage, and communication. For many years, improvements in architecture and technology enabled computers to get smaller and faster without increasing power usage. Unfortunately, although engineers are still making everything smaller, they are having difficulty increasing speed or reducing power use: Computers are hitting the inevitable limits of speed and power constraints.

The transition toward the Internet of Everything raises the stakes on overcoming these challenges. For example, biomedical researchers are exploring multiple promising opportunities to improve people's health and save lives by embedding sophisticated, computer-enabled medical devices inside the body. But for these devices to become widely applicable, computers are needed that do not quickly burn through their batteries

---

[1]G.M. Amdahl, G.A. Blaauw, and F.P. Brooks, Jr., 1964, Architecture of the IBM System/360, *IBM Journal of Research and Development* 87-101.

or throw off heat that could harm the patients they are intended to help. Current technologies are not sufficient to realize all of the important computing applications envisioned for the future.

A History of Innovation from the Niche to the Mainstream

Martonosi described the evolution of research and technologies that are reflected in today's computer architectures. Much of this work, for example, has been informed by DARPA-funded supercomputing research conducted in the 1970s through the 1990s. Although those investments were targeted at niche areas of computer science, experience has proven that sustained government-funded research ultimately trickles into the mainstream; the results of DARPA's supercomputer research investments are central to the architecture of the computers and smartphones we use today. Martonosi noted, "It's a real success story of research that was done, viewed as niche, that later we had to pull it out of our pockets and use it in a much more mainstream way."

Energy use, Martonosi's focal area, is not a new area of computer architecture; in fact, power has been a consideration since the very first computers. Even the developers of ENIAC, the first electronic computer, developed by Mauchly and Eckert in the mid-1940s, paid careful attention to its power use, which was about 150-175 kilowatts.[2] Ever since those early days, when a computer architecture design hit its power limit, there was a new technology to switch to: first there were relays, then vacuum tubes, then bipolar transistors, and then metal-oxide semiconductors. Today, Martonosi said, computer architects are once again facing power limits, but the difference this time is that there is no ready new technology to switch to that would enable computers to increase their productivity without hitting thermal constraints.

Computer architecture research in the 1990s led to several important developments making computers more energy efficient. One is dynamic voltage scaling. Stemming from InfoPad, a DARPA-funded project at the University of California, Berkeley,[3] this innovation enabled a computer to reduce its power supply voltage in order to optimize power use. Dynamic voltage scaling is now standard on every phone and computer. Other technical solutions to power efficiency, also DARPA-funded, include narrow bit-width optimizations and speculation control. These solutions, developed by basic computer science researchers, were also quickly incorporated into product design.

Power modeling is another innovative idea with roots in basic computer architecture research that took place in the 1990s. For the first time, power models allowed architects to evaluate new ideas for optimizing power usage much earlier in the design

---

[2] G. Farrington, 1996, ENIAC: Birth of the Information Age, *Popular Science* (March):74-76.
[3] University of California, Berkeley, "Infopad: Wireless MultiMedia Computing," http://www.wirelesscommunication.nl/reference/chaptr01/dtmmsyst/infopad/infopad.htm, accessed November 18, 2015.

process. As a result, computer architects were able to influence design, and power models became critical to understanding the power–capability trade-offs. Martonosi's early efforts in power modeling were adopted by the computer industry, specifically IBM, becoming part of mainstream computer design.

By the early 2000s, although researchers had been steadily making improvements, they still needed to do more to address power constraints. A big breakthrough came in 2005, with the invention of on-chip parallelism: the addition of more processors to a silicon chip in order to allow a computer to carry out multiple calculations simultaneously. This development enabled more computation with less power usage. At this point, parallelism research and power research, once separate computer science areas, converged, and the joint research led to the invention of computer chips that contain many specialized, heterogeneous processors to carry out the hundreds of computations made by today's devices.[4]

Martonosi explained that the progress from one technological advancement to the next has not always been linear. As on-chip parallelism was integrated into more products, starting in the mid-2000s, computer architects reached back into decades of DARPA- and NSF-funded parallelism research to improve capabilities in this area. Several key projects, such as those focused on shared-memory cache coherence, scalable protocols, and Hydra chip multiprocessors, led directly to technologies now widely used in today's computer servers, network processors, and smartphones. Martonosi said that parallelism, like the early research on supercomputer architectures, is another area in which early government funding of a niche research area has led directly to technologies that are now in wide use.

A Disruptive Moment

Computer architecture straddles hardware, which allows software to operate, and software, which lets us use computers to perform tasks. Today's seismic changes in both hardware and software are creating significant changes in computer architecture as well, said Martonosi: "I see this as an interesting, exciting, and disruptive moment in computer architecture." Devices today are full of computer chips that are high-performing and power-efficient but incredibly complex to program, including processors for audio, video, face recognition, and dozens of other capabilities. Pointing to the diagram of a modern chip, Martonosi noted, "The manual for this chip is 5,000 pages long."

Martonosi raised the concern that the commercial computing industry is unlikely to address fundamental challenges facing computer architecture, for several reasons. First, as other presenters have said, most companies' goals are too short term and modest to

---

[4] J. Li and J.F. Martinez, 2005, Power-performance implications of thread-level parallelism on chip multiprocessors, pp. 124-134 in *IEEE International Symposium on Performance Analysis of Systems and Software, 2005, ISPASS 2005,* doi:10.1109/ISPASS.2005.1430567.

pursue solutions to high-level, crosscutting problems. Also, hardware and software are in most cases developed by different companies, so few companies have a financial motivation to take on the burden of research and development in the no-man's land between them. In addition, individual pieces of software, also designed by different companies, may not work well together when combined on one device (a bit like the Tower of Babel, according to Martonosi). Finally, companies are also unlikely to collaborate with their competition and may not even feel enough market pressure to tackle the problem.

Martonosi said these issues are likely to lead to an increase in software development costs and a decrease in software reliability and security. The U.S. military systems' reliance on computers, which comprise many different software and hardware parts from many different vendors, illustrates the importance of taking up this challenge at a broad level. There are multiple areas ripe for research, Martonosi added. For example, there is a need for solutions that can help manage chip heterogeneity and establish a better balance between communication needs, which dominate device use today, and computational needs. Basic research advances in these areas would support computer architects' important role as mediators between power usage and computation and hopefully usher in a new generation of computers that can be both faster and more energy efficient.

The Winding Path of Wearables

Computers that are small and lightweight enough to be worn on or in the human body—such as the Apple watch, Fitbit, Google Glass, and others—hold tremendous potential for a variety of uses. But the technology behind today's wearable computers has followed a circuitous and at times surprising path through government-funded academic research, the experiments of hobbyists and tinkerers, and commercialization by multinational technology companies. Today's wearables are made possible by myriad component technologies, such as speech recognition, lithium-powered batteries, cloud computing, and innovative architectures that allow computers to be lightweight, low power, and seamlessly integrated into people's daily lives.

Thad Starner, a professor at the Georgia Institute of Technology's College of Computing and a pioneer in the field of wearable computers, delivered a presentation on the history of wearables while himself sporting Google Glass, a breakthrough wearable product he helped to develop.

Why Wearables?

While wearable computers perform many of the same functions as a smartphone or traditional computer, they offer a number of additional advantages. One is that performing a quick task using a wearable computer requires significantly less movement and attention than accessing a laptop or phone that might be across the table or in another room.

Perhaps most relevant to today's busy, multitasking society is that wearing a computer shortens the length of time between intention and action: as soon as you realize a task needs to be done, you can complete it within seconds.

Because wearables are closer to the body, they can also access health information such as temperature or pulse, making them useful for monitoring fitness activities or providing medical alerts. Starner asserted that more advances are expected in the medical fields. Pacemakers, wearable glucose monitors, wearable insulin pumps, and other such devices, for example, could read signals from a patient's body and personalize treatment accordingly. Rehabilitation specialists are looking into wearable robotics, a truly cross-disciplinary field, to help patients recover muscle strength or limb movement after an injury. Of course, Starner noted, giving computers such access to our bodies and our health information means that privacy and data protection are crucial whenever wearable computing is discussed or designed.

Starner also pointed out that fashion is likely to be a significant driver in the development of wearables. To some extent, wearables may get the most traction from first being fashionable, then becoming more functional as they spread and evolve. The most exciting aspect of wearable computing, in Starner's view, is that the industry is really just getting started: "The interaction between man and machine, between the computer and the user, is just getting interesting. I think we'll see more advances in the next 10 years than in all the previous years combined."

From Fiction to Fact

While a number of wearable computing technologies are gaining steam on the commercial market, the history of research and innovation leading up to this point has been a somewhat bumpy road. "In the press, people are suddenly discovering wearable computing. . . and the question I get often is, 'Why now?' There are actually some very good reasons why we could not do this before," Starner said.

People have been envisioning wearable computers at least as long as computers have been around. A 1945 issue of *Life* magazine featured an article titled "As We May Think," in which computer pioneer Vannevar Bush imagined a futuristic device he postulated would someday assist scientists in their work: a forehead-mounted camera used to record experiments on-the-go. At the time, computers were the size of an entire room and photographic technology was still far from its current digital form, but that didn't stop visionaries like Bush from assuming—correctly, in this instance—that wearable computing would eventually become a reality.

Early work on artificial intelligence and virtual reality (such as "Augmenting Human Intellect: A Conceptual Framework" by Douglas Engelbart in 1962 and Ivan Sutherland's Sword of Damocles head-mounted display in 1968) was also built on the assumption that as computers advanced and connected the world, people would be wearing them and they would truly be a part of us. However, although computer interfaces did get smaller and more advanced, largely thanks to DARPA-funded research, they first evolved into the personal computer, away from the body as separate machines.

Starner recounted how he has long tinkered with wearable computing. As a student at MIT in the late 1990s, he created a wearable computer for taking notes more effectively that included goggles, a keyboard that could be held in one hand, and a 1-pound hard drive stowed in a backpack. Starner's homegrown device presaged his eventual involvement in developing Google Glass, a cutting-edge commercial product designed to fulfill a similar need, albeit in a format that is more appealing to the general public than Starner's original bulky apparatus.

The early 2000s saw a significant push toward mobile wearable computing as smartphones took off and displays grew smaller. A key development in the path to Google Glass was the ability to embed the display inside a glass lens, removing the need for clunky goggles. The resulting technology (see Figure 3.1) allows regular people—not only computer scientists or technology hobbyists—to use this intuitive and seamlessly integrated, wearable technology.

Many of the component technologies that enable today's wearables can be traced to research and development advanced or funded by the federal government. A microdisplay pioneered by Hubert Upton at Bell Labs in the 1960s was later further developed by DARPA for use in military helicopters; the U.S. Army also incorporated the microdisplays into wearable computers to increase efficiency and reduce the number of personnel needed for inspecting tanks. NASA, driven by a need for better cameras for its missions, advanced key technologies that were later incorporated into webcams, smartphone cameras, and Google Glass. Sensing, GPS, and speech recognition are other key ingredients of wearable technology that can be traced back to government-funded research.

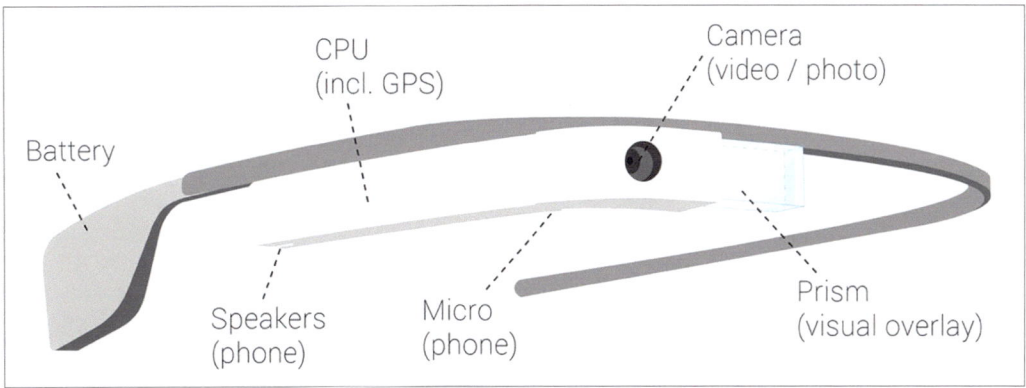

FIGURE 3.1 Google Glass. SOURCE: Martin Missfeldt, "How Google Glass Works," infographic, February 2013, http://www.brillen-sehhilfen.de/en/googleglass, licensed under Creative-Commons-Lizenz CC-BY.

Although many of the early drivers for wearable technologies were rooted in government applications, wearables have clearly had commercial appeal as well. In 1995, Nintendo stuck two microdisplays together and sold 1 million units of its Virtual Boy, the first virtual reality consumer product. Finding no existing standard for personal-area networks and unable to deploy wearables for its employees without such a standard, FedEx convened experts to create the one used today, IEEE 802.15.6.

While wearables might seem, to the casual observer, as if they arrived overnight, Starner stressed that today's consumer wearables could be traced down a long path from the hobbyist researcher and the federally funded lab to military applications to consumer products. As these devices continue to improve and become an ever more integral part of our lives, he concluded, we owe a great debt to the government-funded research pioneers, from all areas of computer science, who created the technologies that enable present—and future—wearables.

4

Developing Smart Machines

Machines, ancient and modern, are tools to serve our needs. For eons they have carried out a huge variety of tasks, from manufacturing goods, to transporting people around, to helping us decipher the natural world, to simply entertaining us. Machines can fight, protect, heal, and even teach us. But what they have not been able to do until quite recently is to learn, make decisions, and act on their own.

Today, intelligent machines are everywhere. From the Netflix recommendation engine to Google Translate to Apple's Siri voice-recognition system, artificial intelligence has become sufficiently accurate, reliable, and useful to find its way into numerous devices and applications. These technologies have taken off in parallel with a dramatic expansion of the amount and complexity of data, which provides fertile teaching ground from which machines can learn to make intelligent decisions on their own.

In the related area of robotics, engineers have made remarkable achievements by combining sophisticated software and artificial intelligence with equally sophisticated hardware to create machines that perform useful tasks in diverse real-world contexts. These robots now provide a variety of valuable services and perform activities that it would be impossible or dangerous for humans to attempt.

This chapter presents an introduction to key concepts in machine learning by Jaime Carbonell of Carnegie Mellon University; a history of artificial intelligence achievements by Eric Horvitz of Microsoft; and an exploration of robotics by Rodney Brooks of ReThink Robotics.

MAKING MACHINES LEARN

Most tasks performed by computers today are the result of traditional programming: Systems are developed to perform specific functions in response to specific inputs in order to fulfill a predetermined set of requirements. But in an increasing number of scenarios, we need computers not only to do the things they are programmed to do, but also to be able to take inputs and tell us something we didn't already know or perform a task we didn't specifically tell them to do—in short, to acquire the skill of learning.

Machine learning is a field that combines artificial intelligence, which is the ability of machines to make intelligent decisions, with data analysis, which allows machines to gain knowledge. There is a great deal of crossover between machine learning and artificial intelligence, and some see machine learning as a subfield within the broader scope of artificial intelligence. Essentially, machine learning is what lets computers discover patterns within data and then use those patterns to make useful, and ideally correct, predictions. Those predictions can then be used to make decisions or take actions that are appropriate for a given situation, the same way a human would.

Jaime Carbonell, a professor of computer science at Carnegie Mellon University and an expert in artificial intelligence and machine learning, presented an overview of the key challenges and approaches involved in machine learning.

How to School a Computer

Machine learning has virtually unlimited economic and consumer applications for fields as varied as medicine, robotics, finance, entertainment, and transportation. "Machine learning essentially is the engine that is driving modern artificial intelligence," said Carbonell. "And the big impact is everywhere." While a traditionally programmed self-driving car might be able to find its way around a city, it takes machine learning in order for a car's driving system to notice another driver's behavior, predict that he or she is about to cut in front of it, and slow down to allow that event to happen safely. By harvesting information from the environment, machines can adapt to our dynamic world to make smarter decisions.

Carbonell described the complex, multistage process of teaching a machine to learn. Central to machine learning is the process of feeding training data into a mathematical prediction model in order to test and refine the model to the point that the machine can use it to acquire and apply future knowledge. A key goal of this continuous learning process, Carbonell explained, is to minimize errors by continually assessing the difference between actual outcomes and predictions made by the machine-learning system. Minimal error is crucial to many machine learning and artificial intelligence applications—for example, when models are used to guide health care decisions or military activities or to design a system for manufacturing airplanes.

To further refine the learning algorithms, engineers must train the machine to appropriately handle and learn from outliers, rather than just typical data. In traditional statistics and engineering applications, researchers seek the most accurate reflection of a data set as whole and try to weed out or de-emphasize rare or extreme cases that do not reflect the norm. In machine learning, on the other hand, researchers cannot ignore rare cases; in fact, it is these outliers that give the machine some of its most important learning opportunities.

For example, machine learning often deals with unbalanced data sets in which the ultimate focus of decision making is precisely the outlier cases. In medicine, very few patients will actually have the rare disease researchers are interested in. In airplane safety, very few flights will result in accidents, yet these present the greatest learning opportunities Therefore, in machine learning, such instances are not mere statistical noise, but central lessons for the system to learn from: If you ignore the outliers, Carbonell said, "you could miss everything that is interesting."

Broadly speaking, machine learning engineers select mathematical models, analyze historical data sets to generate and refine their models, and then apply the models to make predictions about new data. Through this process computers can be developed that use mathematics the way humans use mental models when they encounter a new situation, recognize a pattern, and adapt their behavior to it. In computers, this is known as transfer learning. Along with related theories such as deep neural networks and proactive learning, transfer learning is seen as an important driver for future machine learning advances.

Tapping Big Data

Recent years have seen a surge of progress in machine learning thanks in large part to the rapid growth of big data, the enormous data sets now being generated by thousands of information-sensing devices in both the scientific world and the everyday world. Big data is now integral to every branch of science: "Not everything in the disciplines is big data or data sciences, but data sciences has a part of every single one," said Carbonell. "Data science, which you can loosely define as big data plus machine learning plus domain knowledge, is the big win in this area—their combination is the big win." Because big data sets are large scale, highly complex, and multidimensional, they are extremely difficult to work with. Many layers of computing technologies, such as cloud storage, privacy and security controls, data merging and cleaning algorithms, and other tools and methods are required in order for a big data set to reach a state where analysis can occur.

Only once big data is in this state can it be incorporated into machine learning. Carbonell explained that big data has propelled numerous recent advances in machine learning; on the flip side, it is precisely because we are in an era of big data that we need machine learning systems more than ever. Machine learning has become crucial to the ability to sift through, analyze, and understand today's highly complex data.

Creating the Multilingual Computer

Much of Carbonell's work has focused on imbuing machines with the ability to process natural human language. Reflecting on the history and current state of this field, Carbonell noted that rather than being a linear progression of ideas and methods, the dominant theories in machine-based language translation systems today are the product of a collective development of numerous different theories that have evolved and converged over the years.

In particular, Carbonell identified two key moments in the development of machine translation. The first took place in the mid-2000s, when rule-based language translation systems (which retrieve information from dictionaries and grammar rule sets) were replaced by statistical translation systems (which use statistical models based on the analysis of parallel texts). This transition enabled the invention of Google Translate and similar services, which represented a significant breakthrough, albeit still with relatively high rates of error compared to human expert translations.

A second advance was structural learning. Using structural learning, a system can translate whole language structures, as opposed to individual words or phrases. One of its advantages is that words and sentences can be reordered, even across large chunks of text, creating a smoother, more natural output as opposed to a clunky, word-by-word translation. It is a far more complicated, but more promising, area of research, and Carbonell said ongoing work in this area has already greatly reduced machine translation error rates. And, the combination of structural learning and deep neural networks promises further improvements.

One particularly complex problem facing machine translation today, according to Carbonell, is dealing with rare languages. Uncommon languages create two main hurdles for current machine translation techniques: First, there is generally not a lot of existing data a computer can use to learn the language, and, second, in some cases rare languages have substantially different structures, such as more complex morphology, than more common languages. Yet incorporating rare languages into machine translation is worthwhile, because it could help to preserve rare languages, such as Alaska's Iñupiaq or Greenland's Kalaallisut, and also to make the Internet and the outside world more accessible to speakers of such languages.

Another key challenge is decoding word ambiguity. Carbonell illustrated this challenge by presenting different uses of the seemingly straightforward English word "line." Line can refer to a power line, a subway line, an actor's line in a play, online, or many other meanings, and machine translation systems must use context to decide which meaning is correct. Big data and innovative algorithms are crucial to developing models that can better handle such challenges.

Harnessing the Wisdom of Crowds

Engineering a machine learning system and giving it data to learn from is not sufficient to create a truly intelligent machine. Carbonell pointed out that learning in machines, like learning in people, takes time and tinkering.

He explained that active learning is crucial to this process in which the computer identifies questions or missing data and actively seeks answers or data to fill in the gaps. It is a continuous cycle between a computer and a human that allows the machine to refine its knowledge and understand nuance. In the case of machine translation, for example, the computer attempts a translation, identifies a missing piece of information, and then asks a human to supply it. The machine then incorporates that data, and all the other data gleaned from active learning, into its models to create better and better translations over time.

Instead of one expert supplying data, Carbonell said this function can also be performed by a crowd of nonexperts, which can be a less expensive approach to training a machine using active learning. When working on a translation, for example, the computer would catch an obvious error and solicit suggestions from the crowd. The crowd, offering subtly different translations, cumulatively helps to reduce ambiguities and improve the translation model. The process ultimately results in translations that are better than any single nonexpert in the crowd could create alone. Although machine translation might not be as good as a professional human translator, the large and nuanced body of information created by the crowd helps the machine produce language that is recognizably human. Machine learning is successful, Carbonell noted, because "there's no data like more data." More data bring more learning. Although Carbonell acknowledged challenges to working with a crowd of nonexperts to refine machine translation models, these can be overcome and are worth the excellent training the translation systems receive.

In Carbonell's view, future machine learning research will benefit from both the large increase in available data and the rise of crowdsourcing. Crowdsourcing can work especially well with a crowd of experts. In computational biology, for example, harnessing the collective ideas of multiple biologists has helped to parse complex and variable protein structures or interactions between proteins, tasks that are exceedingly difficult for one person or machine to perform alone but that can provide important insights for the development of new drugs or vaccines.

With the advent of the era of big data, today is an exciting time for machine learning. By taking advantage of new, vast data sets and new modeling techniques, machine learning researchers are making important strides toward intelligent machines that can bring enormous benefits to medicine, education, energy, finance, and society as a whole.

ACHIEVEMENTS IN ARTIFICIAL INTELLIGENCE

The goal of artificial intelligence (AI) is to create computers capable of making decisions that produce a realistic outcome that is as good as or better than the outcome when decisions are made by humans. There are numerous applications of these technologies, and they are largely used to augment or support human activities by going beyond human decision-making capability in some way. In some cases, artificial intelligence enables decision making in situations that are beyond the reach of humans owing, for example, to danger or physical constraints. In other cases, it is used to inform decisions that require more data than any human could access or process alone.

The idea that machines could be built to think like humans is as old as computers themselves. Eric Horvitz, managing director of Microsoft Research's main Redmond laboratory and an expert in artificial intelligence, presented an overview of the history and primary achievements of artificial intelligence research and development.

Creating the Theoretical Foundation

Although the term "artificial intelligence" was not coined until the 1950s, an important predecessor field, known variously as operations research or decision science, blossomed in the 1940s and laid much of the groundwork for the birth of artificial intelligence. Operations researchers studied analytical methods to create models that aid in decision making. Building on this context, John McCarthy, one of the co-founders of artificial intelligence, coined the term in a 1956 proposal to pursue work related to forming abstractions, self-improvement, manipulating words, and developing a theory of complex intelligences. Notably, these are still active areas for artificial intelligence research today.

Horvitz described the development of artificial intelligence in the years since as a multisector, cooperative process spanning decades. "This has been a very shared, collaborative process across industry and academia with great funding from the agencies," he said. After branching away from operations research in the late 1950s, artificial intelligence researchers became particularly interested in logic, searching, and finding acceptable but not necessarily optimal, results (known as "satisficing") to make decisions. Although this divergence narrowed the focus of artificial intelligence somewhat, it also led to significant innovation.

In the mid-1980s, the field went through another transformation focused on how to handle uncertainty. Unknowns are inherent in any system, and dealing with these creates pressures in artificial intelligence, such as how to make decisions in high-stakes scenarios or within realistic constraints, how to learn in an environment where data keep increasing, and how to interact with real people in the real world. Opting to reduce their emphasis on resolving uncertainty altogether, researchers in this period became more focused on using artificial intelligence to solve specific problems. In one DARPA-funded study, for example, paramedics used artificial intelligence–enabled devices to receive real-time advice while treating a patient in crisis (see Figure 4.1). One important outcome of this early research was what are known as "approximations." When a patient is gasping for breath, there is not enough time to run through every possible reason why this is happening and create a subsequent care plan; using approximations allows a system to compute decisions and determine each outcome quickly and coherently.

These theoretical and methodological advances were driven largely by government funding, Horvitz explained. Over time, numerous federal agencies have been interested in pursuing artificial intelligence for a variety of applications, from health to space exploration. Agencies including the National Science Foundation (NSF), the Office of Naval Research (ONR), the National Library of Medicine (NLM), and the National Aeronautics and Space Administration (NASA) greatly advanced the field in its early days, in Horvitz's view, through targeted funding of early artificial intelligence and machine learning research.

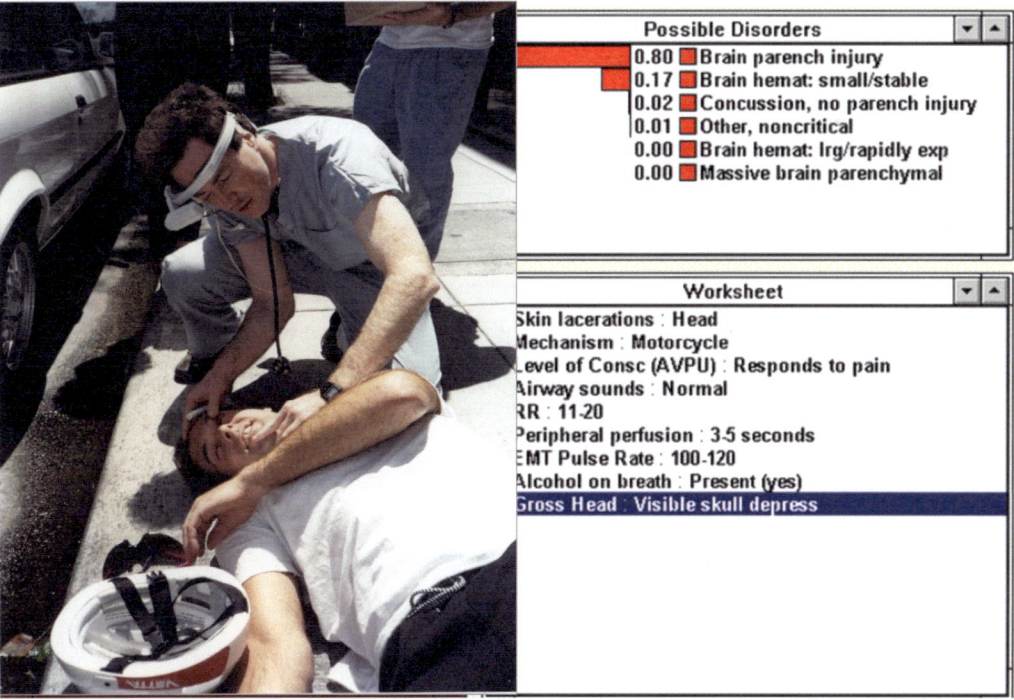

FIGURE 4.1 AI-enabled devices used in a medical crisis. SOURCE: E. Horvitz and M. Shwe, Handsfree decision support: Toward a non-invasive human-computer interface, *Proceedings of the Annual Symposium on Computer Applications in Medical Care,* 1995:955, 1995. Courtesy of Eric Horvitz, Technical Fellow and Managing Director at Microsoft Research.

Impacts and Achievements of Research on Intelligent Machines

This early, government-funded artificial intelligence research had an enormous impact, not just on technology but also directly on the U.S. economy. In the 1990s, pairing artificial intelligence research with the growth of the Internet enabled the creation of e-commerce, a crucial driver of today's economy. For example, about 20 years ago researchers started working on what is now known as "collaborative filtering." This artificial intelligence fuels the recommender engines on websites like Netflix and Amazon—the "you might also like" suggestions that propel a significant proportion of e-commerce activity. Researchers with the inclination—and funding, largely from government sources—played an instrumental role in developing and refining collaborative filtering, enabling the eventual commercial applications that we depend on today.

Other key achievements in artificial intelligence that can be traced to early government-funded research include computer-aided perception, language, and movement tracking. Horvitz described how research funded by DARPA and other agencies followed a clear path to today's face recognition technology, now used in myriad applications including military intelligence and national security, crime-fighting, and consumer uses. Today's artificial intelligence systems can process and match data based on images of faces as well as auxiliary information such as location, events, and even clothing.

As techniques for perceiving visual cues and understanding language became more refined, these developments also paved the way for teaching machines how to track and understand human movement. Research in this area led directly to consumer products like the Xbox Kinect and Nintendo's Wii, which track and respond to the body's movements. To artificial intelligence researchers, Horvitz said, these products seem shockingly inexpensive considering the enormous amount of hard work and innovation that led to their invention.

Another key innovation rooted in artificial intelligence research is stacked representation, also known as neural networks. Although this modeling approach emerged in the late 1980s, there were not enough data available at the time for neural networks to make accurate predictions. With the rise of big data and today's data-intensive scientific methods, together with conceptual advances in how to structure the networks, neural networks have reemerged as a useful way to improve accuracy in artificial intelligence models. They have been applied, for example, to reduce the error rate in speech recognition systems. These advances enabled many innovations, such as the Skype real-time translation service, which, Horvitz said, "would stun our colleagues 10 or 15 years ago."

Since Horvitz's early experience with the DARPA-funded project to provide artificial intelligence support for paramedics, the field has advanced numerous applications in health care, including increasing hospitals' ability to predict readmissions and allowing doctors to perform surgery remotely, a technique known as telesurgery (see Figure 4.2).

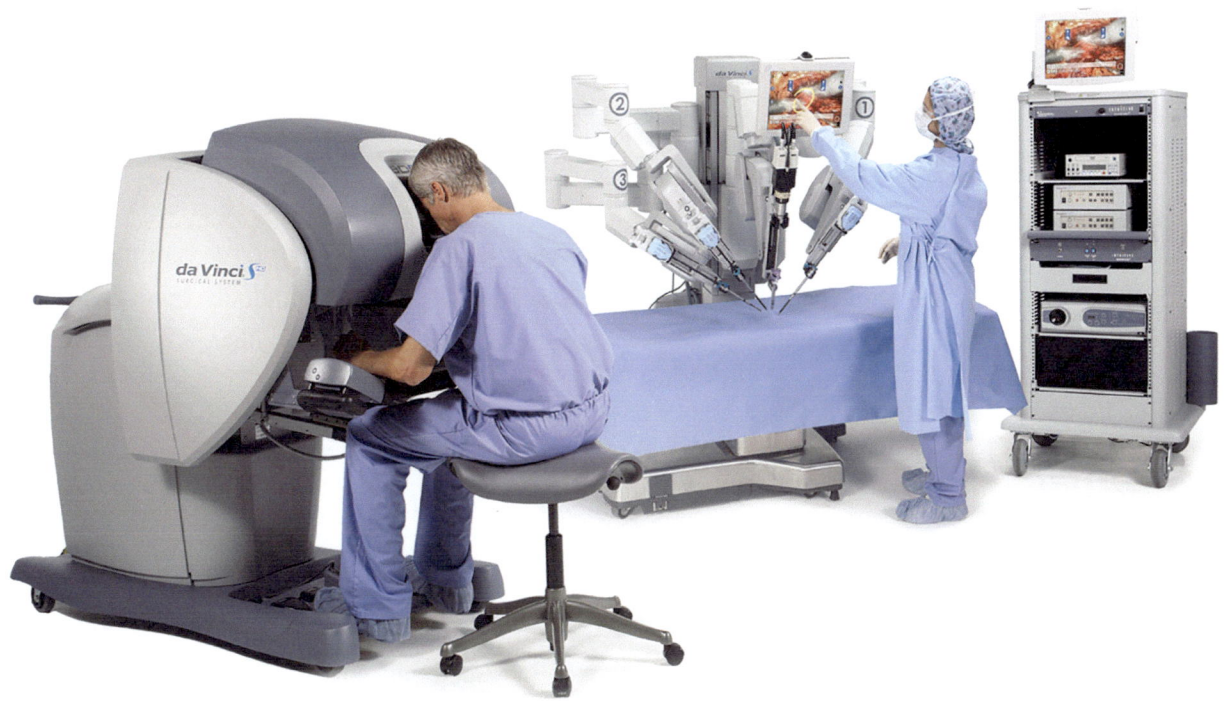

FIGURE 4.2 Full da Vinci S surgical system. SOURCE: Courtesy of Intuitive Surgical, Inc.: Full da Vinci S Surgical System, ©2016 Intuitive Surgical, Inc.

Successful telesurgery research, funded by DARPA, enabled researcher Phil Green at SRI to create Intuitive Surgical, a company of substantial value specializing in methods that enable minimally invasive surgery through robotics and artificial intelligence. "It's stunning what the DARPA investment could do," reflected Horvitz.

Promising Prospects for the Future

Today, artificial intelligence work continues to advance through collaborations among industry labs and federal agencies. For example, work by Microsoft and Google, building on advances funded by DARPA, has led directly to technologies we now use daily, including grammar checking and personal assistants like Siri and Cortana. In transportation and infrastructure, artificial intelligence work has been applied to improve wind maps for aviation and urban traffic modeling, among many other things.

Future artificial intelligence research, Horvitz predicted, will likely include enhancing vehicle safety, improving self-driving cars, and improving the ability of computers to answer deeper questions. Human–machine collaboration, in which a problem is divided into two parts, one given to a computer and one to a human to work on together, also holds great promise. For example, a surgical approach in which a machine and a human work together could bring huge benefits to patients and medical staff.

Horvitz identified augmented cognition, where machine learning complements human cognition in areas such as memory, attention, or judgment, as another exciting research area. Integrative artificial intelligence, or the creation of systems that can interact with the complexity of real-world settings, also holds great promise. Integrative artificial intelligence, said Horvitz, could be the key to transforming computers, which currently have deep but very narrow intelligence, into broader, more humanlike thinking machines.

It is clear from Horvitz's many examples that government-funded artificial intelligence research has reaped many benefits for the technology sector, the economy as a whole, and our everyday technologies. Continued research will no doubt bring future rewards in this promising and fast-evolving field, Horvitz said.

ROBOTICS: FROM VISION TO REALITY

Robotics is another area in which engineers have made remarkable gains in developing machines that can operate independently and make smart decisions. Today's robotics achievements reflect a strong government–industry–consumer pipeline that has had important impacts on science, industrial manufacturing, and our everyday lives.

Rodney Brooks has long been at the forefront of this field. Among the earliest pioneers of robotics, Brooks has seen his work go to Mars and into people's kitchens. His work at Stanford University in the 1970s, funded by NASA, focused on creating simple mobile robots. At the time, creating robots also required that one either invent or implement needed components such as stereo vision, map building, and planning. At the time, creating a robot able to move 20 feet by itself over the course of 6 hours was considered a huge victory. As today's Martian rovers and vacuuming robot Roombas make clear, we have come a long way.

SLAM Dunk

According to Brooks, one of the most crucial innovations that propelled robotics into the field as it is known today is SLAM (Simultaneous Localization And Mapping). SLAM is an essential skill for robots: it is what gives them the ability to enter an unfamiliar environment, map it, and understand their own place within that map. Remarkably, two papers presented at the same conference in 1985, one by Brooks and his team at MIT and one from a laboratory in France, trying to solve the same problem independently, led to SLAM's creation.[1] After the conference, the two teams' work was disseminated across the robotics research community.

---

[1] R.A. Brooks, 1985, Visual map making for a mobile robot, pp. 824-829 in *1985 IEEE International Conference on Robotics and Automation, Proceedings,* doi:10.1109/ROBOT.1985.1087348; R. Chatila and J.-P. Laumond, 1985, Position referencing and consistent world modeling for mobile robots, pp. 138-145 in *1985 IEEE International Conference on Robotics and Automation, Proceedings,* doi:10.1109/ROBOT.1985.1087373.

SLAM turned out to be key to solving many thorny robotics issues, and by 1991 the academic research community had collectively made significant improvements on initial SLAM approaches. This process, said Brooks, illustrated how the community inspires itself and propels research forward, from one federally funded idea to another. It also showed how making a hardware prototype, however imperfect, freely available for others to tinker on moved robotics from a nebulous theoretical area to a series of well-defined research problems that scientists could then collectively solve. Initially the bulk of this work was led by federally funded labs at Stanford, MIT, and the University of Pennsylvania; by the mid-1990s, many more researchers were working on further improvements.

Some initial robotics projects were funded by DARPA, NASA, and NSF for applications in defense, space, and science, respectively, but the consumer products industry also benefitted from this research. In fact, the self-driving Google car and other high-end cars with highly computerized functioning are direct descendants of SLAM and DARPA-funded research. Federal Grand Challenge and Urban Challenge grant programs were specifically launched to drive innovation and progress on functional autonomous vehicles; industry then took SLAM out of the labs and put it on real roads. "There's a long history, from the late 1970s to now, of an idea that wasn't about self-driving cars when it started—it was about navigation on other planets," reflected Brooks.

Learning from Nature

Of course, robots do not only need to understand and map their environments; they also need to physically navigate them. Stuck on the problem of improving robots' ability to navigate the rough and unpredictable terrain on other planets, Brooks turned to an approach known as behavior-based robotics. In behavior-based robotics, engineers use the natural movements of creatures such as insects, spiders, and birds to inspire new robot structures and ways of moving (see Figure 4.3). These approaches, for example, can improve a robot's ability to right itself if knocked over or avoid getting stuck in crevasses. After some early success based on these new robotics models, Brooks was awarded NASA funding that enabled him to develop the Mars Rover.

The success of the Mars Rover encouraged Brooks to start his own private company to build robots, iRobot. In this capacity, he continued to develop robots for government applications; for example, DARPA funded work to create robots to search for and dispose of improvised explosive devices (IEDs) in Iraq and Afghanistan. The company also pursued consumer-oriented robots, including the Roomba, a robot vacuum that has sold 14 million units (and inspired countless YouTube videos of cats riding Roombas).

One story from iRobot's early days illustrates the serendipity of innovation and just how difficult it is to predict when a research project might go from the theoretical to the practical. In the mid-1990s, the Japanese government provided iRobot some initial fund-

FIGURE 4.3 Hexapod robot. SOURCE: Courtesy of Burhan Saifullah.

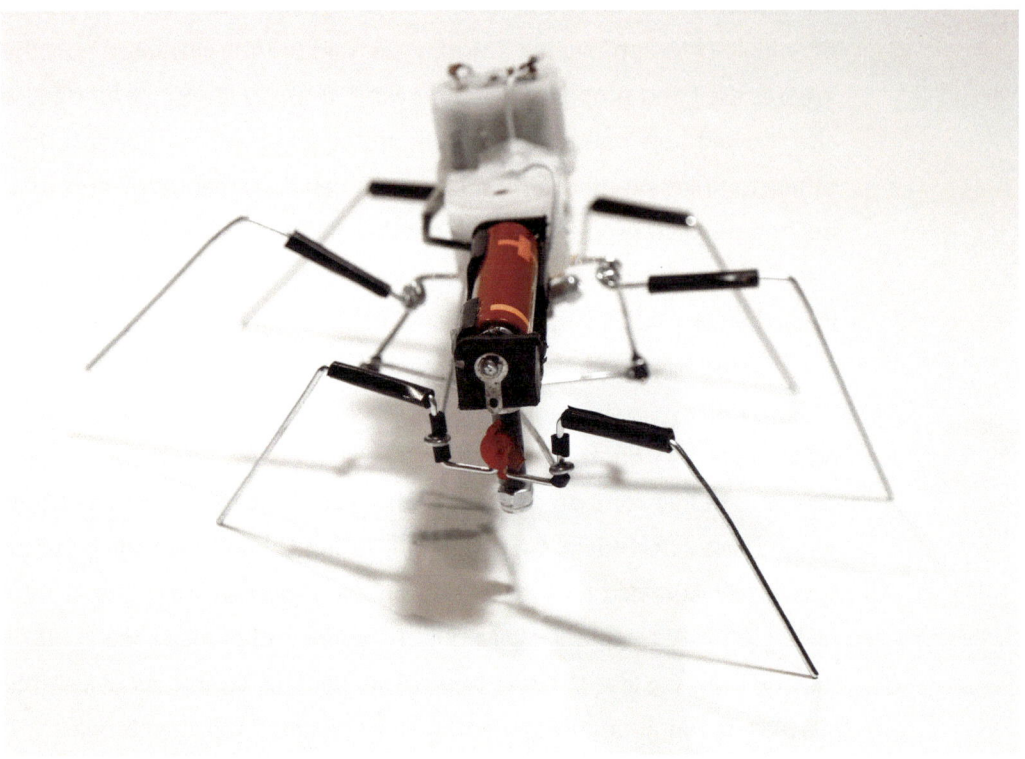

ing to begin developing robots to support operations in Japanese nuclear power plants. The project was later aborted after the Japanese government decided the robots would not be needed. Two decades later, when the 2011 Fukushima nuclear reactor meltdown rendered the plant too unsafe for people to enter, iRobot's battle-hardened IED disposal robots were called upon to enter the plant and survey the damage.

Cultivating a Softer Side

Brooks highlighted the fact that research advances in humanoid robotics have also made it easier for robots to be deployed in factories among people. He explained that before recent improvements in user interfaces and robotic design, factories had to separate their human employees from the robots used in manufacturing processes. The robots, with their complicated user interfaces, awkward movements, and enormous size, were too dangerous for most people to work with. Today's humanoid robots allow factory workers with no scientific or robotic expertise to easily and safely train and monitor their robotic partners (see Figure 4.4).

These industry robots, now ubiquitous in thousands of manufacturing facilities, can trace their lineage back to agencies like DARPA and NASA, which, despite not knowing exactly what the outcomes would be, led the way toward key robotics breakthroughs by funding basic research in the field's early days. Without this initial early government funding, robotic factories and self-driving cars would likely still be mere mirages on the far-off horizon.

Despite today's remarkable technological capabilities, however, we still have a long way to go before we can use some of these technologies to their fullest potential. The adoption of driverless cars and trains, for example, will require not just better technology but also more trust and acceptance on the part of the public, Brooks explained. The 2009 crash of a self-driving Metro train in Washington, D.C., set social acceptance of autonomous vehicles back despite being a more efficient way to run subway lines. It is often the case, he said, that even when a new technology is ready for the consumer market, the consumers might not be ready for it.

Sharing their own perceptions of the field, several attendees noted that robotics research really took off once mobile robot-building platforms became inexpensive enough that every lab could afford one. Instead of a few teams working on research problems, suddenly there were dozens or hundreds of teams actively building off of each other's innovations, and the field thrived. While government-funded research was clearly crucial for the field's beginnings, Brooks noted, it is the ongoing synergy of research funding, academic labs, and industry products that continues to fuel innovation.

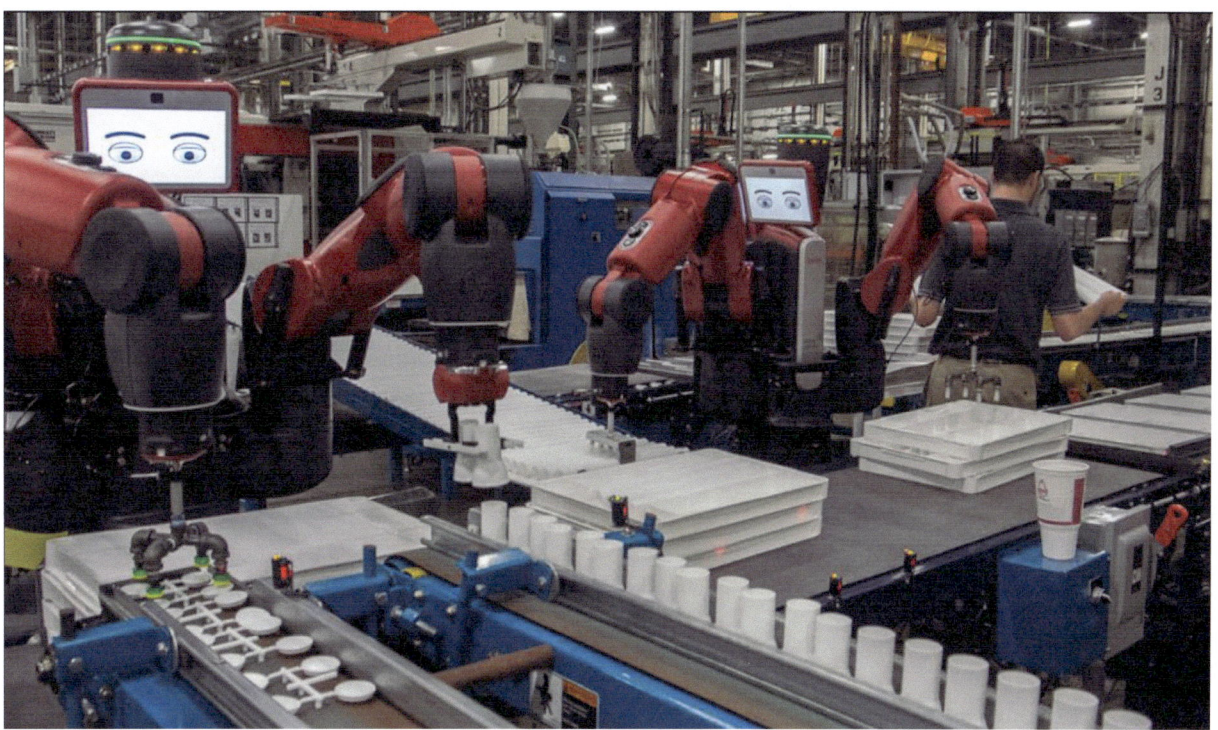

FIGURE 4.4 Industrial assembly robots. SOURCE: Courtesy of Rethink Robotics, Inc.

5

People and Computers

As all of the workshop presenters made clear, computers and communications technologies have had a profound impact on everyday lives and will continue to do so in the foreseeable future. A common thread of the workshop was the constant push and pull between technology and people: the ways people influence technology and, in turn, the ways technology influences people. This chapter focuses on three presentations exploring different aspects of the relationships between humans and technologies: cybersecurity, user-centered design, and social science research.

In his presentation, Stefan Savage shared key challenges and trends in cybersecurity. In the next presentation, Scott Hudson described the emergence and key contributions of user-centered design in computer science. A basic premise of user-centered design is that no matter how innovative or elegant a new program or piece of hardware is, technology sinks or floats based on how useful—and usable—it is. Drawing examples from academic research and commercial products, Hudson described the practice of user-centered design and its crucial role in the success of many of the technologies depended on today. The third presentation, by Duncan Watts, explored how technology has been informed by—and has itself opened up vast new opportunities for—social science. Insights about how people behave and interact with each other are of tremendous value for businesses and governments alike, and Watts described how this research has been fueled by a strong government–academia–industry ecosystem.

SEEKING CYBERSECURITY

While much of the workshop focused on the positive outcomes of the many technological innovations that have been enjoyed over the past few decades, Stefan Savage discussed a darker aspect of this technological growth: cybersecurity. Savage, a computer science professor and researcher at the University of California, San Diego, has spent his career working on cybersecurity topics such as network worms, malware, and wireless security.

Defining "security" as freedom from fear and danger, Savage described how technological changes have brought both new fears and new dangers. He attributed most of today's security challenges to five major developments: the Internet and its pervasive connectivity, e-commerce, data centralization, mobile technologies, and the emergence of the Internet of Things. In short, Savage said, "We have handed over control of our lives to computers and to the networks that interconnect them."

What makes cybersecurity such a pernicious problem, he explained, is that it is not merely a technological challenge that can be "fixed." Because cyberattackers are human and stand to gain financially from these activities, it is actually a socioeconomic problem with adversaries, victims, and defenders. Technology simply provides the tools and setting for these battles to unfold.

Another key challenge, according to Savage, is that "we have no way to evaluate security solutions except by how they fail." This confusion leads to a morass in the cybersecurity field with many problems but few solutions.

Savage discussed how cybersecurity is also a crosscutting discipline. The challenge for this field has long been how to build security solutions into the entire array of quickly-developing technologies and applications, from machine learning algorithms to wearable computers and personal monitors to robots and autonomous vehicles.

Savage traced many of the major components of cybersecurity in use today to 30 years of federally funded academic research. Thanks to government funding, academic researchers not only were able to focus on developing individual security solutions for individual problems but also had the time and funding to incorporate cybersecurity research into larger public policy problems. This government funding has spurred industry-wide advances in cybersecurity that extend far beyond the reach of one specific product or technology.

Rather than delving into the long history of computer security, Savage focused on two recent stories that illustrate how government-funded academic cybersecurity research has been essential in creating industrywide standards that protect consumers and businesses. The first story, from the automobile industry, led to safer cars, and the second story, relating to software piracy, helps businesses protect intellectual property.

Security in Transportation

Although most people may not be aware of it, Savage said transportation today is "deeply computerized." A single car, for example, may have up to 30 different computers all networked together, from the radio to the brakes to the air conditioning (see Figure 5.1). Many of these computers are designed to provide functions that humans cannot; for example, adjusting the fuel-oxygen mixture to regulate emissions. Others enhance safety or provide entertainment. The net result is a huge amount of digital information being created and transmitted by incredibly complicated systems; yet, most in-car computer systems are equipped with far fewer security protections than a typical personal computer.

Savage's research has shown that it is possible to tap into these systems to remotely take over a car. In one experiment, for example, his team was able to deactivate the brakes of a brand new car, straight off of the dealer's lot, from 1,000 miles away using several undefended virtual access points.

Savage pointed out that the car industry has some "extra-technical" challenges that make incorporating cybersecurity especially difficult. Car manufacturing is a complex process involving numerous third-party suppliers; many of the component computers that wind up in a single car come from different manufacturers and use different programming languages, making it difficult to secure both the component parts and the car as a whole.

FIGURE 5.1 Computers in the modern automobile. SOURCE: Courtesy of Karl Koscher and Stefan Savage.

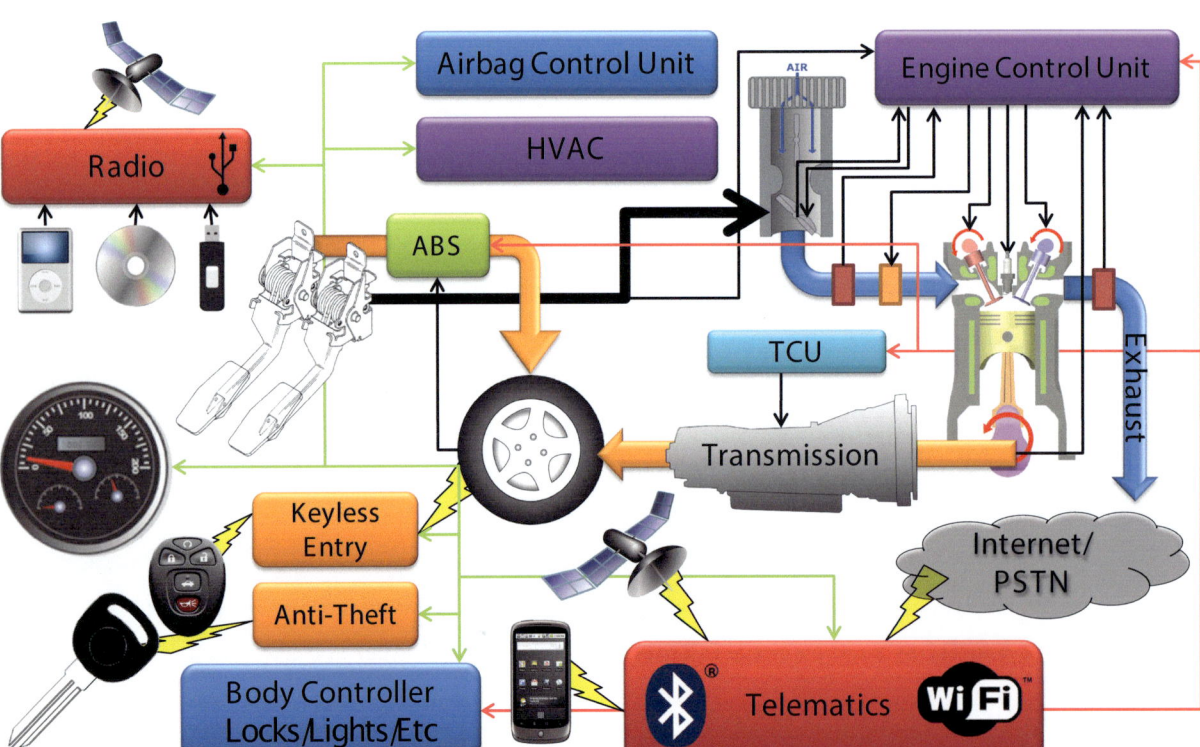

In addition, in many cases the systems are so complex that traditional cybersecurity tools do not apply. "If you bought an American car in the last few years, it probably has a phone number and an Internet address," said Savage. "There are lots of good reasons why it has that, but the side effect is that we now have this kind of systemic risk."

Cars are just one example of the broader trend toward the "Internet of Things," in which computers and connectivity are being built into many types of products beyond typical computer products like laptops and smartphones. This trend is especially active in the area of transportation. "There is almost no trip that you take, whether it is up or down a floor or whether it is through the air, that you are not ultimately depending on a computer to do the right thing," said Savage. Anything with computer control and connectivity is subject to risk, whether it is a car, airplane, train, or refrigerator. Yet the companies that make these products do not feel the same pressure to increase their security as do companies that make traditional computer products; because no one is known to be attacking such products, companies have so far made only modest security investments.

But there is good news. By exposing weaknesses, research by Savage and others has propelled a wholesale overhaul of how the American auto industry designs software. Savage noted that this was not something that would have been advanced by the private sector alone; only academic researchers had the time and long-term vision to unravel these problems, work with regulators and industry leaders, and convince the National Transportation and Safety Board that these were pressing problems requiring industrywide solutions and standards. Even after new security standards and recommendations were in place, Savage said that the auto industry might have been tempted to ignore them, except for the fact that around the same time, Toyota was forced to pay more than $1 billion in fines because of its "unintended acceleration" problems.[1] This quantified a previously unquantifiable problem for the auto industry by revealing what a security breach could cost them. In Savage's view, the prospect of future enormous payouts scared industry into finally adopting the cybersecurity standards that had been developed by academia with government support.

Fighting Spam and Piracy

Whereas cars and other computerized devices are examples of an underappreciated cybersecurity threat, industry and the general public have a much greater awareness of the problems of spam and piracy. In particular, the sale of pirated software is a particularly active problem and one that the software industry spends hundreds of millions of dollars to stem.

Savage described an innovative approach his team developed to fight Internet spammers selling pirated software. Until recently the traditional approach has been to filter

---

[1]C. Woodyard, 2012, Toyota to pay $1.1B in 'unintended acceleration' cases, *USA Today,* December 26, http://www.usatoday.com/story/money/cars/2012/12/26/toyota-unintended-acceleration-runaway-cars/1792477/.

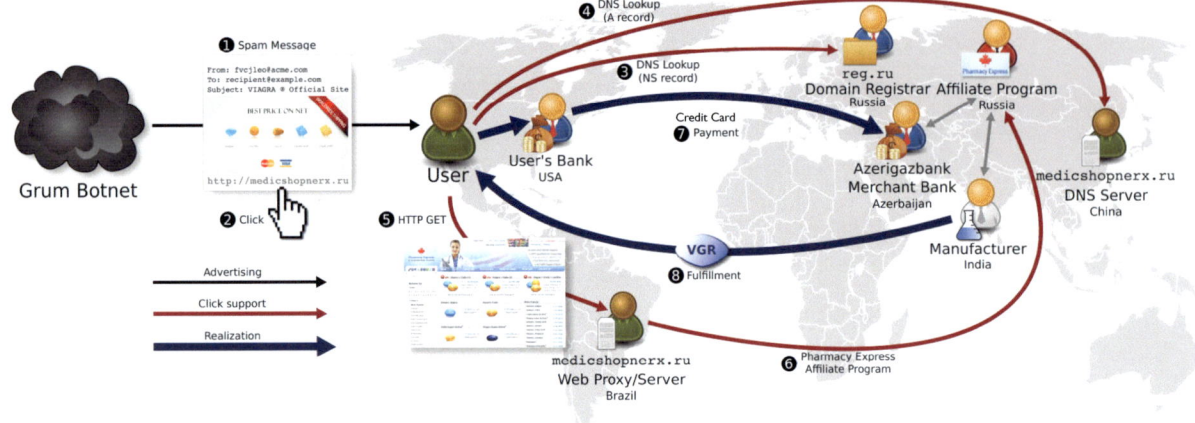

FIGURE 5.2 Spam e-mail complex value chain. SOURCE: K. Levchenko, A. Pitsillidis, N. Chachra, B. Enright, M. Félegyházi, C. Grier, T. Halvorson, et al., Click trajectories: End-to-end analysis of the spam value chain, pp. 431-446 in *2011 IEEE Symposium on Security and Privacy,* doi:10.1109/SP.2011.24. Courtesy of Christian Kreibich.

spam emails, shut down websites hawking pirated software, and seize any goods. But this approach rarely solves the problem permanently, because the same spammers can easily pop up again using new e-mail and web addresses (see Figure 5.2). Also, the spam system works in large part because there is consumer demand for cheap pirated software. "Up to 40 percent of all revenue from e-mail spam comes from people who go into their Spam folder and click on the items there, because they want those things," Savage said.

Given this challenging context, Savage and his team approached the problem from a different angle. Realizing that it's a game being played for financial gain, they tried to find a way to undermine the finances of the software pirates. Targeting e-mail spam as just one symptom of the larger problem of piracy, the team untangled the complex connections going from the e-mail offer, to the web proxy, to the domain server and several other points along the way until getting to the actual financial processing. In order to undermine spammers' financial gains, Savage's team purchased more than 600 items from spam e-mails (using no government money, Savage noted, though the research was otherwise government-funded), and followed the processing chain to determine how the spammers were receiving their money. The study revealed that 95 percent of the money acquired through pirated software spam was going through just three banks.[2]

Once alerted to the penalties of working with spammers, the banks quickly dropped these accounts, leaving spammers with no way to monetize their sales. While

---

[2] C. Kanich, N. Weavery, D. McCoy, T. Halvorson, C. Kreibichy, K. Levchenko, V. Paxson, G.M. Voelker, and S. Savage, 2011, Show me the money: Characterizing spam-advertised revenue, pp. 219-234 in *Proceedings of the 20th USENIX Conference on Security* (SEC'11), USENIX Association, Berkeley, Calif.

switching e-mails or domains is easy, switching banks is far more difficult for spammers, and this strategy has proved effective in shutting down certain types of spammers. As a result, there has been a substantial drop in sales of pirated software as a whole, and the process of targeting spammers' finances is now widely used by virtually all companies looking to protect their intellectual property from unauthorized distribution.

In computerized cars and software piracy and on numerous other cybersecurity fronts, Savage said academia has a crucial role to play and that solutions cannot be left to industry or government alone. With government funding, academic researchers have the ideal funding structures and culture to experiment with strategies before their value is obvious. Companies and mission-oriented government agencies, on the other hand, are often crisis-focused and unable to invest in the long-view, experimental solutions cybersecurity requires. This critical, government-funded academic work has exposed weaknesses in consumer products and bolstered the intellectual property rights of businesses, said Savage—and our citizens and our economies are safer because of it.

THE USER-CENTERED DESIGN RENAISSANCE

Scott Hudson, a professor of human–computer interaction at Carnegie Mellon University, presented an overview of the evolution and spread of user-centered design and its impacts on the adoption and success of technology. Although it's easy to assume this approach was a foregone conclusion, he described how computer scientists spent decades working hard behind the scenes in order to "make it easy to make things easy."

The enormously successful photo-sharing application Instagram, developed by a team of two, gained 30 million users over a 2-year period until being acquired by Facebook for $1 billion. Although it's an extreme example, this story illustrates the enormous value of user-centered design in the creation of software products: Ease-of-use was critical both to the meteoric rise of Instagram among consumers and to the ability for such a small team to develop and quickly deploy such a wildly successful app.

In the early days of the personal computer and the Internet, using software to perform even relatively simple tasks took knowledge and experience. Today, most software is designed to be so intuitive to the user that there is virtually no learning curve involved. But the benefits of user-centered design do not stop with the user: Software developers and the technology industry as a whole have benefitted from this trend as well. Where it used to take experienced developers weeks or months to create the user interface for a new software tool, now nearly anyone can create technology applications quickly, easily, and well, even with minimal technical skills.

Building Toward a Sea Change

Computer scientists were not initially focused on user-centered design. In the 1980s, many academic researchers were working on simplifying computer programming, but from a top-down, systems-level perspective. The user—the person who would ultimately interact with the software to perform tasks—was an afterthought. Early academic research projects such as Tiger[3] and ADM[4] were intended to simplify user interfaces but were too systems-focused; these and other processes born of academic research were clunky and complicated for nonexperts.

It was from this context that a gradual sea change emerged in the 1980s and 1990s, creating a growing recognition that computer science needed to be user-centered, not systems-centered, in order to succeed. More and more, people began to realize that the solution to clunky, difficult software would come not from a new technology or algorithm, but from a new approach to design altogether.

This new user-centered mindset, although ultimately the key to the success of many technologies and companies, complicated everything. Even compared to the programming required to make a highly complex computer system work, figuring out the user's needs and preferences is an extremely tricky challenge. "Users are hard to deal with, because you can't open the user's head and pour in the right mental model," said Hudson. Recognizing that creating something that can be used is the fundamental end goal for computers, computer scientists had to come to terms with the fact that you must design for the users you actually have, not the users you wish you had, he added.

Hudson described how the first generation of developer-friendly toolkits for creating user-friendly interfaces emerged from exchange and interplay between academic researchers at places like Carnegie Mellon, Stanford, and MIT and companies such as Sun, Apple, and Microsoft. In the 1990s, three major projects led by Linton at Stanford, Myers at Carnegie Mellon, and Hudson at the University of Arizona and Georgia Tech created functional user interface design toolkits including Interviews and Fresco, Garnet and Amulet, and Artkit and subArctic, respectively. Contributions from these projects, such as concurrency models, resizable icons, and layout abstractions, are evident today in Apple, Android, and Adobe user tools.

Another successful tool coming out of that era was graphic user interface builders—programs that allow developers to actually draw the graphical parts of a graphical user interface instead of creating them only with lines of code. These visual tools were a big success and led to what is now a maxim of user-centered design: "Visual things

---

[3]D.J. Kasik, 1982, A user interface management system, *Computer Graphics* 22(4):113-120.

[4]A.J. Schulert, G.T. Rogers, and J.A. Hamilton, 1985, ADM—A dialogue manager, pp. 177-183 in *Proceedings of SIGCHI Conference on Human Factors in Computing Systems* (CHI '85), Association of Computing Machinery, New York, N.Y.

should be expressed visually." Today, every modern development environment has visual components. Microsoft even used the term "visual" in a series of programming products: Visual Basic, Visual C++, and Visual Studio.

A New Way of Creating Technology

Once user-centered design became a more universal and widely accepted part of the technology development process, more innovations followed. "Now we see the fingerprints of this work all over modern interactive systems of all sorts," reflected Hudson.

One important example of early user-centered design research was Columbia University's 1997 Touring Machine project, in which researchers experimented with deploying, in real-world situations, mobile computing contraptions that included a computer with wireless Internet access, GPS, and a handheld display and input (Figure 5.3). The machines, despite being impractical, were an essential part of the user-interaction research that laid the groundwork for mobile devices to come. Building and using them helped researchers explore how people might use a mobile device with Internet connectivity, and the project's devices are seen as important early precursors to the iPhone.

FIGURE 5.3 Prototype 3D mobile augmented reality.
SOURCE: S. Feiner, B. MacIntyre, T. Hollerer, and A. Webster, A touring machine: Prototyping 3D mobile augmented reality systems for exploring the urban environment, pp. 74-81 in *First IEEE International Symposium on Wearable Computers,* 1997, doi:10.1109/ISWC.1997.629922. Courtesy of Steven K. Feiner.

Another example, from a subarea of user-centered design focused on interaction techniques, is the "pinch" gesture: a smooth interaction for simultaneous translating and scaling text or an image. While it may seem new, this feature actually traces its roots to Myron Kruger's 1983 VideoPlace gaming system. The zoomable interface was invented in 1994, and adding zoom to the pinch gesture allows users to maximize space and readability on the small screens of today's smartphones and wearable devices.

In Hudson's view, these and many other innovations, enabled by the major cultural shift away from systems-focused design and toward the user, were significant drivers behind today's "There's an app for that" world. In less than 10 minutes, as opposed to days, weeks, or months not so long ago, a novice can now create a working app and start accumulating users and revenue. "Computing has now spread out into lots of places it hasn't been before, . . . [so] it has had a tremendous impact that we haven't seen before," said Hudson.

Taking a user-centered approach has led computer scientists to change the questions that they ask when conceptualizing a new product, explained Hudson. Instead of wondering if they can build a technology, or how to start building it, following a user-centered approach means asking, "How well does it work with the user?" User-centered design has been revolutionary for many applications and areas of computer science, including wearable computing, context-aware computing, and data visualization.

A general lesson from the story of user-centered design, Hudson explained, is that rather than investing in research to develop only individual technologies, it is important to target work that has an amplifying effect across the broader field. "Even more than lots of individual technologies, things like this—ideas that amplify other ideas and enable other ideas—are really what we should be after," he said.

While it is impossible to predict at the outset which research project will lead to the next industry-wide innovation, there is still a great deal of room for improvement in user experience and other crosscutting areas of computer science. In the user-centered design space, for example, Hudson said high-performance computing could be made much more accessible with simple, user-friendly tools. Such tools could enable nonscientists, such as small business owners, to learn more from the specialized data they collect.

The mindset change from a top-down, systems view of computer design to a user-centered view has had an enormous impact across multiple technologies and the technology-driven economy in general, mostly by amplifying the impact of technologies and by making them easier to develop. In Hudson's view, user-centered design is an idea that then inspires other ideas, but there was no direct path or single research project that led to this epiphany. Rather, it took a winding path and even some seeming dead ends to gradually build into a sea change that enabled the flexible, user-friendly tools and technologies we enjoy today.

HARNESSING BIG DATA FOR SOCIAL INSIGHTS

Technological developments over the past several decades have opened up powerful new opportunities for understanding people and societies. New ways of generating, collecting, and analyzing social data have shed new light on economics, politics, sociology, anthropology, and many other areas within the social sciences. Research into the questions posed by these fields touches every aspect of human society, from families and interpersonal relationships to high-stakes topics like presidential elections, international politics, and economic markets.

Government funding has long been central to enabling new insights in these areas. Duncan Watts, a principal researcher at Microsoft Research, offered his views on how the online world has changed social science, the emerging importance of computational science as a way to understand and solve social science research questions, and the role of the government–academia–industry ecosystem in advancing this field. Watts began his research career in mathematics but quickly became fascinated by the dynamics of connections and networks among people and has conducted research at Columbia University, Yahoo! Research, and other organizations. At Microsoft, he studies the social networks that dominate today's online culture.

From Social Science to Social Media (and Back Again)

Watts described how federal funding has been instrumental in laying the groundwork for a whole new sector of the economy: the online social world. To the casual observer, it is easy to assume that wildly popular social media companies like Facebook and BuzzFeed simply stumbled upon winning formulas for connecting and engaging their users. In reality, Facebook and other social networks are built, in part, on research from the early 2000s examining the drivers of network structure, network growth, and social contagion, while BuzzFeed and other news sites build from research on the nature of social influence to tailor their articles to what readers are most likely to enjoy and share with friends, Watts explained. In addition to underpinning such applications in the for-profit sector, Watts said fundamental research on networks and relationships is also being integrated into basic and translational research in other areas of science, such as medicine, physics, and biology.

Conversely, just as the social sciences helped to fuel the growth of social media, social media are providing new fodder to advance social science research. Now that online social networks are thriving, Watts and other researchers in government, academia, and industry are tapping into this new online world and its data to further study human networks and social problems.

A New Way to Do Research

Social scientists have long studied "off-line" social networks, but in the past there was no easy way to harness large amounts of social and behavioral data, and data collection was often a painstaking and time-consuming process. "If you're trying to understand how information flows through a society, you need to know what people think, you need to know when they change their minds, you need to know whom they are talking to. This is a tremendous observational challenge when you are talking about millions of people," said Watts. Now, with people constantly interacting with media and each other through technologies capable of recording and storing their behavior, researchers are making progress far more quickly. "We realized after [the invention of social networks] that this is a tremendous wealth of information that can inform us about social interaction and behavior," said Watts.

In particular, online surveys and crowdsourcing tools such as Mechanical Turk have made it easier for researchers to connect with research subjects and gather data. For example, researchers can now take advantage of the "bored at work" network—people who are constantly on computers and willing to fill out surveys as a brief distraction from their daily tasks—to quickly and cheaply gather survey data. In addition, the emergence of virtual meetings has made it more feasible for researchers to study group dynamics because it is no longer necessary in every case to gather people together in the same room at the same time.

One of the most powerful aspects of social media for social science is that data can be collected passively, without relying on information that is actively solicited through surveys or focus groups. Because the use of social networks is so widespread and users of these services are generating so much data, social science is increasingly becoming a computational science, in which researchers tap extremely large data sets for insights about people's behavior. "It's clear to us working in the field now that social science over the last decade or so is rapidly becoming a computational science," said Watts, adding that the use of high-performance computing has benefited greatly from the interplay between government-funded academic research and industry data and tools. Watts said, "I think it's also very clear that both federal funding and support from industry labs have been critical."

Watts highlighted a handful of examples of how social media and online networks have shed light on human behavior. For example, one NSF-funded study Watts's group conducted in the mid-2000s, when he was at Columbia University, showed how social media can create a snowball effect in which the perceived popularity of an item influences more people to like it. The study revealed that the more popular a previously unknown song appeared to be (as indicated by how many "likes" it had), the more popular it became, while songs with fewer "likes" were basically ignored.[5] So, although we tend to assume that we make our own decisions about our purchases and preferences, people are more subject to others' tastes than we think. The study provided valuable evidence that the consumer market doesn't merely reveal preferences but can construct them through a process of social influence.

In an earlier study, Watts and his collaborators used email to replicate Stanley Milgram's famous "small world" experiment, which determined that there are a median of six degrees of separation between people. The NSF-funded study achieved the same results as Milgram's, revealing that people could reach a stranger, even across the globe, through a chain of 5-7 contacts, on average (see Figure 5.4).[6]

---

[5] M. Salganik, P. Dodds, and D. Watts, 2006, Experimental study of inequality and unpredictability in an artificial cultural market, *Science* 311:854-856.

[6] P. Dodds, R. Muhamad, and D. Watts, 2003, An experimental study of search in global social networks, *Science* 301(5634):827-829.

FIGURE 5.4 Milgram's six degrees of separation experiment replicated by e-mail.
SOURCE: Duncan J. Watts, "From Small World Networks to Computational Social Science," presentation to the workshop, March 5, 2015, http://sites.nationalacademies.org/cs/groups/cstbsite/documents/webpage/cstb_160426.pdf.

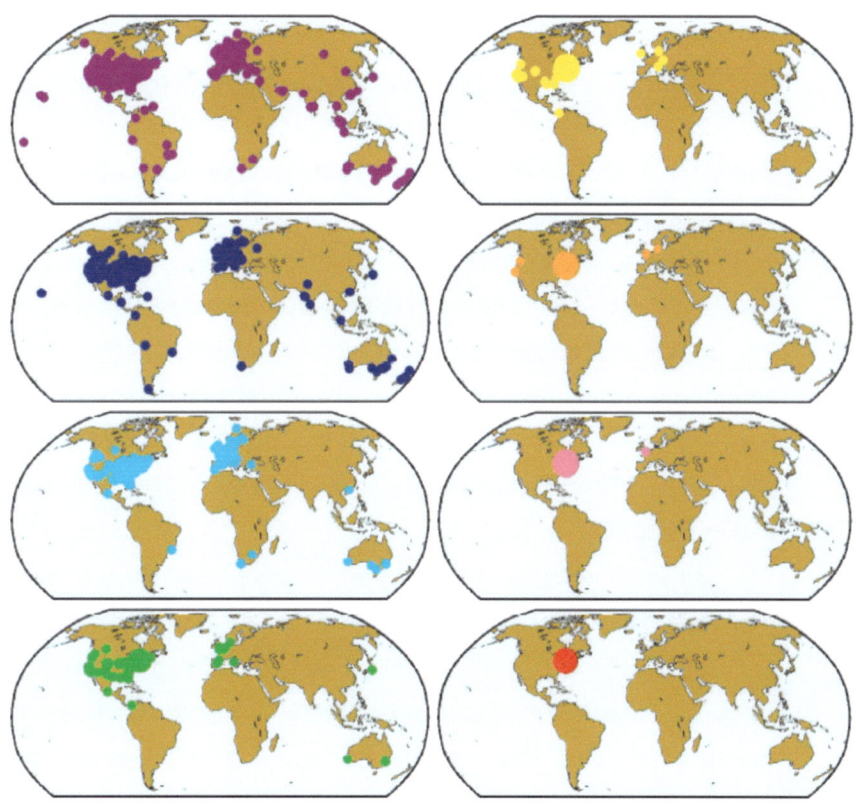

A more recent study, which Watts oversaw in his current position at Microsoft Research, tracked information dissemination on Twitter and attempted to quantify and categorize what makes news items "go viral" on social networks.[7]

Social media hold virtually limitless potential for insights into human behavior; further applications of these data, for example, include crisis mapping, the real-time gathering and analysis of social media information during a political crisis or natural disaster, and digital ethnography, the study of relationships in a digital rather than a physical space. In addition, Watts said smartphones offer fertile ground for research and could be used as "social sensors" or to mine data on productivity. The thousands of data points being generated by smartphones and all of our other interactive technologies hold "profound implications for what we could know about the state of the world, what we could know about the collective mind, what we could do in terms of interventions, peer influence, and collective behavior or crowd computing," said Watts.

---

[7] S. Goel, A. Anderson, J. Hofman, and D. Watts, 2015, The structural virality of online diffusion, *Management Science* 1-17.

A Prolific Data Ecosystem

Social science is an area in which the government–academia–industry ecosystem is particularly evident. Watts pointed out that while most social science research is supported by the government, much of the data used in these studies is generated by companies. The technology industry is also funding and advancing research, not merely providing the data—particularly in the area of computational research in which large data sets are mined for insights. Yahoo! Labs, for example, conducts its own research while also making data sets freely available for academic use.

The marriage of computer science and social science will be crucial to advancing the next generation of social science questions and solutions, Watts said, adding that both federal and industry funding will be critical to this effort. Looking back, Watts admitted that he never would have expected to see an online social network capable of reaching a billion people, yet this has come to pass. As this example shows, it is impossible to predict what will be available 10 or 15 years from now, even for experts embedded in the field.

Although reluctant to make specific predictions given this inherent uncertainty, Watts said a likely key to future social science insights will be an increasing trend toward interdisciplinary work. Social science is interdisciplinary by nature, yet social scientists and computer scientists often work separately in academic departments with little overlap. A greater emphasis on more interdisciplinary, mixed-method research focused on solving problems, not just publishing papers in journals, will be important to keeping social science research moving both forward and sideways into other scientific fields, said Watts.

Finally, Watts noted that the push-and-pull between humans and technologies becomes ever more critical to understand as the computing world moves closer to the human world. As robotic technologies become more integrated into our lives and wearable computers literally become a part of us, new approaches to computer design will be needed in order to fully understand the needs of the user and design the best possible solutions. This is a key area in which interdisciplinary work uniting social science, user-centered design, and computer science will be crucial to advancing effective solutions.

6
Wrap-Up Discussion

This chapter sums up some of the discussions presenters and attendees had at the workshop. In a relatively short time, technology has transformed the human experience from the personal and familial to the level of entire societies and economies. Looking back over the tremendous technological achievements of the past several decades, some participants said it might be tempting to imagine that each advancement built on its predecessor and laid the foundation for the capabilities to follow. Indeed, to a casual observer, it might seem logical, even inevitable, that the personal computer led to the laptop, the smartphone, and the smart watch, or that the first computer-to-computer connection led to the Internet, to cellular networks, and to Wi-Fi.

However, as one workshop attendee pointed out, innovation does not automatically follow innovation like dominoes set on end. Rather, innovation is a messy, unpredictable, and at times convoluted process. Ideas emerge, diverge and converge, blossom and wither, only to reemerge in unexpected places decades later. Each step—from personal computer to laptop, from laptop to smartphone—requires radically new architectures, new hardware and batteries, new software and user interfaces, new ways to store and transmit information. And powering it all is an incredible amount of human ingenuity.

Given the long list of research organizations, including the federal, academic, and industrial entities mentioned over the course of the workshop, it was pointed out that none of the outcomes could have been achieved by a single company, research enterprise, or government. As another participant put it, nearly every component of every incremental technological innovation has its roots in the complex interplay among fundamental research and development in federal agencies and universities and further research, development, and deployment by private-sector companies.

In some cases, such as the early development of the Internet, as highlighted in Cerf's presentation and the "tire tracks" graphic, the relationship among these players can be roughly visualized as a pipeline, starting with a visionary government funding program, which in turn powers academic research, which then generates insights or technologies that are ultimately adopted for commercial use by industry. In other cases, such as the parallel progress of social science and social media, advances emerge from an interwoven, interdependent ecosystem in which government and academic research and industry data and tools alternately build off of each other.

At the heart of each of the stories presented at the 2015 Continuing Innovation in Information Technology workshop lies a common theme: Several workshop attendees could not imagine that today's incredible technological landscape would have emerged as quickly or as fully had it not been for the rich body of work conducted with government funding. Discussions among some workshop attendees highlighted that industry clearly has played a crucial role in applying, scaling, and commercializing technologies and has even conducted a good deal of early research and development. But the incentives and funding structures that drive industry are not sufficient, alone, to support the highly experimental, uncertain, and broad-based basic research that lays the foundation for truly revolutionary innovations. From critical infrastructure such as the Internet to techniques and regulations that support cybersecurity, government and government-funded research has played a central role in the development of the vast majority of computer science methods and tools that we depend on today.

As discussed by Jahanian, when the government funds computer science research to fuel engineering innovations, the costs are shared by the U.S. population. So, too, are the benefits. Several other examples presented during the workshop, including advances in the use of big data, intelligent machines, and robotics, government-supported technology innovations have supported our military and national security, fueled our global leadership in science and medicine, helped empower citizens as a whole, and enriched the economy. The benefits of industry investment in technology research and development, too, extend not only to the people

> [I]ndustry clearly has played a crucial role in applying, scaling, and commercializing technologies and has even conducted a good deal of early research and development. But the incentives and funding structures that drive industry are not sufficient, alone, to support the highly experimental, uncertain, and broad-based basic research that lays the foundation for truly revolutionary innovations.

who can afford to buy the commercial products they create, but also our own military and government, as well as the economy as a whole.

The nation stands on the brink of yet new transformations. As discussed by Horovitz and Brooks, recent developments make it feasible to envision that robots will, in the not-so-distant future, routinely work alongside humans to rescue, protect, and serve us. That self-driving cars, trains, and planes will regularly deliver us safely to our destinations. That new types of immersive, responsive digital environments will instruct and amuse us. And that many of us will benefit from sophisticated devices worn in and on our bodies to support our health and well-being.

As noted by several attendees, the technologies of the past and present suggest that all of the innovations envisioned for the future—as well as those we cannot yet imagine—will likely emerge not from the genius of one person or one company, but from a complex, symbiotic cycle between government-supported long-term application-engaged research alongside industry-driven solutions and applications. Tomorrow's technologies, like innovations past, are not a foregone conclusion. To realize envisioned innovations—and even to maintain access to the technologies already relied on—there are substantial obstacles in terms of the hardware, software, the infrastructure, and society itself. For innovation to thrive, it is crucial to cultivate the entire government–academia–industry ecosystem that supported this field in the past and that is essential to driving it forward into the future.

Appendixes

A

Committee Biographies

PETER LEE, *Chair,* is a computer scientist and technology innovator at Microsoft Corporation. As corporate vice president, Dr. Lee's mission is to create research-powered technologies and products for Microsoft, while at the same time advancing human knowledge through the open dissemination of fundamental research. He leads the company's New Experiences and Technologies group (MSR NExT), a global organization that conducts R&D in a wide range of technology areas. Recent scientific contributions and technology innovations from NExT include advances in deep neural networks for computer vision, as well as the simultaneous language translation feature in Skype; new silicon and postsilicon computing technologies; experimental undersea data centers; next-generation augmented-reality experiences for HoloLens and virtual reality devices; and large-scale sociotechnological experiments such as XiaoIce and Tay.

    Dr. Lee joined Microsoft in 2010 as distinguished scientist and managing director of the Microsoft Research Redmond laboratory and later took on leadership of Microsoft's U.S.-based research operations, comprising seven laboratories and more than 500 researchers, engineers, and support personnel. Before joining Microsoft, he held key positions in government and in academia. His most recent position was at the Defense Advanced Research Projects Agency (DARPA), where he founded and directed a major technology office that supported research in computing and related areas in the social and physical sciences. One of the highlights of his work at DARPA was the DARPA Network Challenge, which mobilized millions of people worldwide in a hunt for red weather balloons—a unique experiment in social media and open innovation that fundamentally altered how the Department of Defense thought about social networks. Before DARPA, Dr. Lee served as head of Carnegie Mellon University's (CMU's) computer science department, top-ranked in the nation. He also served as the university's vice provost for research. At CMU, he carried out research in software reliability, program analysis, security, and language design. He is well-known for his codevelopment of proof-carrying code techniques for enhanced software security and has tackled problems as diverse as programming for large-scale modular robotics systems and shape analysis for C programs. Dr. Lee is a fellow of the Association for Computing Machinery (ACM) and serves the research community at the national level, including policy contributions to the President's Council of Advisors on Science and Technology and membership of both the National Academies of Sciences, Engineering, and Medicine's Computer Science and Telecommunications Board and the Advisory Council of the Computer and Information Science and Engineering Directorate of the National Science Foundation (NSF). He was the former chair of the Computing Research Association and has testified before both the U.S. House Science and Technology Committee and the U.S. Senate Commerce Committee. Dr. Lee holds a Ph.D. in computer and communication sciences from the University of Michigan, Ann Arbor, and bachelor's degrees in mathematics and computer sciences, also from the University of Michigan, Ann Arbor.

MARK DEAN is the John Fisher Distinguished Professor at the University of Tennessee (UT) College of Engineering. His research focus is advanced computer architecture (beyond Von Neumann systems), data-centric computing, and computational sciences. Before joining UT, Dr. Dean was chief technology officer, Middle East and Africa, for IBM and an IBM fellow. In this role he was responsible for technical strategy, technical skills development, and exploring new technology-based solutions for the region. These responsibilities include the development of solutions specific to the emerging needs of the businesses and cultures in industry segments such as mobile services (banking, health care, education, government), natural resource management (oil, gas, mining, forest, water), cloud-based business services, and security (fraud protection, risk management, privacy, cybersecurity). Dr. Dean was also vice president World Wide Strategy and Operations for IBM Research. In that role, he was responsible for setting the direction of IBM's overall research strategy across eight worldwide labs and for leading the global operations and information systems teams. These responsibilities include management of the division's business model, research strategy, hiring, university relations, internal/external recognition, personnel development, innovation initiatives and the division's operations. During his career, Dr. Dean has developed all types of computer systems, from embedded systems to supercomputers, including testing of the first gigahertz CMOS microprocessor, and establishing the team that developed the Blue Gene supercomputer. He was also chief engineer for the development of the IBM PC/AT, ISA systems bus, PS/2 Model 70 & 80, the Color Graphics Adapter in the original IBM PC, and holds three of the nine patents for the original IBM PC. One invention—the Industry Standard Architecture (ISA) "bus," which permitted add-on devices like the keyboard, disk drives and printers to be connected to the motherboard—would earn election to the National Inventors Hall of Fame for Dr. Dean and his colleague Dennis Moeller. Dr. Dean's most recent awards include National Institute of Science Outstanding Scientist Award, member of the American Academy of Arts and Sciences, member of the National Academy of Engineering (NAE), IEEE fellow, Black Engineering of the Year, the University of Tennessee COE Dougherty Award, member of the National Inventor's Hall of Fame, and recipient of the Ronald H. Brown American Innovators Award. Dr. Dean received a B.S.E.E. degree from the University of Tennessee in 1979, an M.S.E.E. degree from Florida Atlantic University in 1982, and a Ph.D. in electrical engineering from Stanford University in 1992.

EDWARD FRANK is cofounder and CEO of Brilliant Lime, Inc., and Cloud Parity, Inc., both social/mobile software firms. Previously, Dr. Frank was a vice president at Apple, Inc., and corporate vice president for research and development at Broadcom. Before becoming corporate vice president of R&D, he co-founded and led the engineering group for Broadcom's Wireless LAN business, which is now one of Broadcom's largest business units. Dr. Frank joined Broadcom in May 1999 following its acquisition of Epigram, Inc., where he was the founding CEO and executive vice president. From 1993 to 1996, he was a co-founder and vice president of engineering at NeTpower, Inc., a computer workstation manufacturer. From 1988 to 1993, Dr. Frank was a distinguished engineer at Sun Microsystems, Inc., where he co-architected several generations of Sun's SPARCstations and was a principal member of Sun's Green Project, which developed the precursor to the Java(tm) cross-platform web programming language. Dr. Frank holds more than 40 issued patents. He is a University Life Trustee of CMU and a member of its board's executive committee. He received a B.S.E.E. and an M.S.E.E. from Stanford University and a Ph.D. in computer science from CMU.

YANN LeCUN is director of artificial intelligence research at Facebook and Silver Professor of Computer Science at the Courant Institute of Mathematical Sciences. He is the founding director of the New York University (NYU) Center for Data Science and holds appointments as professor of neural science with the Center for Neural Science and professor of electrical and computer engineering with the ECE Department at NYU/Poly. In 1987, Dr. Lecun joined Geoff Hinton's group at the University of Toronto as a research associate. He then joined the Adaptive Systems Research Department at AT&T Bell Laboratories in Holmdel, New Jersey, in 1988. In 1991, he spent 6 months with the Laboratoire Central de Recherche of Thomson-CSF in Orsay, France. Upon his return to the United States, he rejoined Bell Labs. Shortly after AT&T's second breakup in 1996, he became head of the Image Processing Research Department, part of Larry Rabiner's Speech and Image Processing Research Lab at AT&T Labs-Research in Red Bank, New Jersey. In 2002, he became a fellow of the NEC Research Institute in Princeton. Dr. LeCun joined the Courant Institute of Mathematical Sciences at NYU as a professor of computer science in 2003. He was named Silver Professor in 2008. In 2013, he became the founding director of the NYU Center for Data Science. Dr. LeCun has been associate editor of *PLoS ONE*, *International Journal of Computer Vision*, *IEEE Transactions on Pattern Analysis and Machine Intelligence*, *Pattern Recognition and Applications*, *Machine Learning Journal*, and *IEEE Transactions on Neural Networks*. Since 1997, he has served as general chair and organizer of the Learning Workshop, held every year since 1986 in Snowbird, Utah. He is also a member of the Science Advisory Board of the Institute for Pure and Applied Mathematics, University of California, Los Angeles. Dr. LeCun has given numerous invited talks at various international conferences and workshops. He has published more than 180 technical papers and book chapters on machine learning, computer vision, robotics, pattern recognition, neural networks, handwriting recognition, image compression, document understanding, image processing, VLSI design, and information theory. His handwriting-recognition technology is used by several banks around the world, and his image compression technology, called DjVu, is used by hundreds of websites and publishers and millions of users to access scanned documents on the web. An image recognition model he devised, convolutional network, is used by such companies as Facebook, Google, Microsoft, NEC, Baidu, and AT&T/NCR for products and services such as image recognition and tagging, document recognition, intelligent kiosk, and other applications. Dr. LeCun is the recipient of the 2014 IEEE Neural Network Pioneer Award, awarded by the Computational Intelligence Society. He received a diplôme d'ingénieur from the Ecole Superieure d'Ingénieur en Electrotechnique et Electronique (ESIEE), Paris, in 1983, a diplôme d'etudes approfondies (DEA) from Université Pierre et Marie Curie, Paris, in 1984, and a Ph.D. in computer science from the same university in 1987.

BARBARA LISKOV is an institute professor at the Massachusetts Institute of Technology (MIT). Dr. Liskov's research interests include distributed systems, replication algorithms to provide fault-tolerance, programming methodology, and programming languages. Her current research projects include Byzantine-fault-tolerant storage systems and online storage systems that provide confidentiality and integrity for the stored information. Dr. Liskov is a member of the NAE, the National Academy of Sciences, and the National Inventors Hall of Fame (inducted in 2012). She is a fellow of the American Academy of Arts and Sciences and the ACM and a charter fellow of the National Academy of Inventors. She received the ACM Turing Award in 2009, the ACM SIGPLAN Programming Language Achievement Award in 2008, the IEEE Von Neumann medal in 2004, and a lifetime achievement award from the Society of Women Engineers in 1996. In 2003, Dr. Liskov was named one of the 50 most important women in science by *Discover Magazine*. Dr. Liskov received a B.A. in mathematics from University of California, Berkeley, and M.S. and Ph.D., both in computer science, from Stanford University.

ELIZABETH MYNATT is the executive director of the Institute for People and Technology (IPaT), a College of Computing professor, and director of the Everyday Computing Lab. Themes in her research include supporting informal collaboration and awareness in office environments, enabling creative work and visual communication, and augmenting social processes for managing personal information. She is also one of the principal researchers in the Aware Home Research Initiative; investigating the design of future home technologies, especially those that enable older adults to continue living independently as opposed to moving to an institutional care setting. Dr. Mynatt is an internationally recognized expert in the areas of ubiquitous computing and assistive technologies. Her research contributes to ongoing work in personal health informatics, computer-supported collaborative work and human-computer interface design. She is a member of the SIGCHI Academy, a Sloan and Kavli research fellow, and serves on Microsoft Research's Technical Advisory Board. Dr. Mynatt is also a member of the Computing Community Consortium, an NSF-sponsored effort to engage the computing research community in envisioning more audacious research challenges. She has published more than 100 scientific papers and chaired the CHI 2010 conference, the premier international conference in human–computer interaction. Before joining the Georgia Institute of Technology faculty in 1998, she was a member of the research staff at Xerox PARC, working with the founder of ubiquitous computing, Mark Weiser. Her research is supported by multiple grants from NSF, including a 5-year NSF CAREER award. Other honorary awards include being named the Top Woman Innovator in Technology by *Atlanta Woman* magazine in 2005 and the 2003 College of Computing's Dean's Award. Dr. Mynatt earned her B.S. (summa cum laude) in computer science from North Carolina State University and her M.S. and Ph.D. in computer science from Georgia Tech.

B

Presentations

Introduction and Welcome, *Peter Lee, Microsoft Research, Chair*

Robotics, Automation, and the Future of Transportation, *Rodney Brooks, ReThink Robotics*

Usability, Human Factors, and Social Computing

Moderator: Beth Mynatt, Georgia Institute of Technology

From Small-World Networks to Computational Social Science, *Duncan Watts, Microsoft Research*

There's an App for That: How We Got Here and Where to Take It, *Scott Hudson, Carnegie Mellon University*

History of Wearables, *Thad Starner, Georgia Institute of Technology*

Computer Architecture, Hardware, and Systems

Moderator: Barbra Liskov, Massachusetts Institute of Technology

Computer Architecture and the Path of Parallelism and Power Research, *Margaret Martonosi, Princeton University*

The Crucial Role of Government Funding for IT, *Robert Colwell, Intel (retired)*

Machine Learning and Artificial Intelligence

Moderator: Peter Lee, Microsoft Research

Data Sciences = Big Data + Machine Learning + Domain Expertise, *Jaime Carbonell, Carnegie Mellon University*

Investments and Outcomes in AI: Paradigm Shifts and a Renaissance, *Eric Horvitz, Microsoft Research*

Communications

Evolving the Internet, *Vint Cerf, Google, Inc.*

The Once and Future Internet of Everything, *David Culler, University of California, Berkeley*

The Wireless Future: Dreams and Challenges (and How Will This Research Impact Technology), *Andrea Goldsmith, Stanford University*

Cybersecurity Research: Stories from the Trenches, *Stefan Savage, University of California, San Diego*

Value of Research Funding for Innovation

Application Engaged Research, *Deborah Estrin, Cornell Tech*

Unleashing the Discovery and Innovation Ecosystem, *Farnam Jahanian, Carnegie Mellon University*

C

Presenter Biographies

RODNEY BROOKS is a robotics entrepreneur and founder, chairman, and CTO of ReThink Robotics (formerly Heartland Robotics). He is also a founder, former board member (1990-2011), and former CTO (1990-2008) of iRobot Corp. Dr. Brooks is the former director (1997-2007) of the Massachusetts Institute of Technology (MIT) Artificial Intelligence Laboratory and then the MIT Computer Science and Artificial Intelligence Laboratory. He received degrees in pure mathematics from the Flinders University of South Australia and a Ph.D. in computer science from Stanford University in 1981. He held research positions at Carnegie Mellon University (CMU) and MIT and a faculty position at Stanford University before joining the faculty of MIT in 1984. He has published many papers in computer vision, artificial intelligence, robotics, and artificial life. Dr. Brooks served for many years as a member of the International Scientific Advisory Group of National Information and Communication Technology Australia and on the Global Innovation and Technology Advisory Council of John Deere & Co. He is currently an Xconomist at Xconomy and a regular contributor to Edge. Since June 2014, he has been a member of the Visiting Committee on Advanced Technology at the National Institute of Standards and Technology. Dr. Brooks is a member of the National Academy of Engineering (NAE), a founding fellow of the Association for the Advancement of Artificial Intelligence (AAAI), a fellow of the American Academy of Arts and Sciences, a fellow of the American Association for the Advancement of Science (AAAS), a fellow of the Association for Computing Machinery (ACM), a fellow of the Institute of Electrical and Electronics Engineers (IEEE), a corresponding member of the Australian Academy of Science, and a foreign fellow of the Australian Academy of Technological Sciences and Engineering. Among his awards are the following: the Computers and Thought Award at the 1991 International Joint Conference on Artificial Intelligence, the IEEE Inaba Technical Award for Innovation Leading to Production (2008), the Robotics Industry Association's Engelberger Robotics Award for Leadership (2014),and the 2015 IEEE Robotics and Automation Award. He has been the Cray lecturer at the University of Minnesota, the Mellon lecturer at Dartmouth College, and the Forsythe lecturer at Stanford University. He was cofounding editor of the *International Journal of Computer Vision* and is a member of the editorial boards of various journals, including *Adaptive Behavior, Artificial Life, Applied Artificial Intelligence, Autonomous Robots,* and *New Generation Computing.* He starred as himself in the 1997 Errol Morris movie "Fast, Cheap and Out of Control," named for one of his scientific papers.

JAIME CARBONELL is a university professor and the Allan Newell Professor of Computer Science at CMU. Dr. Carbonell joined the CMU community as an assistant professor of computer science in 1979 and went on to become a widely recognized authority in machine translation, natural language processing, and machine learning. He has invented a number of well-known algorithms and methods during his career, including proactive machine learning and maximal marginal relevance for information retrieval. His research has resulted in or contributed to a number of commercial enterprises, including Carnegie Speech, Carnegie Group, and Dynamix Technologies. In addition to his work on machine learning and translation, Dr. Carbonell also investigates computational proteomics and biolinguistics—fields that take the computational tools used for analyzing language and adapt them to understanding biological information encoded in protein structures. This process leads to increased knowledge of protein–protein interactions and molecular signaling processes. His career has had an enormous impact on both CMU and the School of Computer Science. He created the university's Ph.D. program in language technologies and is co-creator of the Universal Library and its Million Book Project. He founded CMU's Center for Machine Translation in 1986 and led its transformation in 1996 into the Language Technologies Institute, which he currently directs. He has advised more than 40 Ph.D. students and authored more than 300 research papers. Before joining the CMU faculty, Dr. Carbonell earned bachelor's degrees in mathematics and physics at MIT and a master's degree and a Ph.D. in computer science at Yale University.

VINTON G. CERF is vice president and Chief Internet Evangelist for Google, Inc.. He is responsible for identifying new enabling technologies and applications on the Internet and other platforms for the company. Widely known as a "Father of the Internet," Dr. Cerf is the co-designer, with Robert Kahn, of TCP/IP protocols and basic architecture of the Internet. In 1997, President Clinton recognized their work with the U.S. National Medal of Technology. In 2005, Dr. Cerf and Dr. Kahn received the highest civilian honor bestowed in the United States, the Presidential Medal of Freedom. It recognizes the fact that their work on the software code used to transmit data across the Internet has put them "at the forefront of a digital revolution that has transformed global commerce, communication, and entertainment." From 1994-2005, Dr. Cerf served as senior vice president at MCI. Prior to that, he was vice president of the Corporation for National Research Initiatives (CNRI), and from 1982-86 he served as vice president of MCI. During his tenure with the Defense Advanced Research Projects Agency (DARPA) from 1976-1982, Dr. Cerf played a key role leading the development of Internet and Internet-related data packet and security technologies. Since 2000, he has served as chairman of the board of the Internet Corporation for Assigned Names and Numbers (ICANN), and he has been a visiting scientist at the Jet Propulsion Laboratory since 1998. He served as founding president of the Internet Society (ISOC) from 1992-1995 and was on the ISOC board until 2000. Dr. Cerf is a fellow of the IEEE, ACM, AAAS, the American Academy of Arts and Sciences, the International Engineering Consortium, the Computer History Museum, and the NAE. Dr. Cerf has received numerous awards and commendations in connection with his work on the Internet, including the Marconi Fellowship, Charles Stark Draper award of the NAE, the Prince of Asturias award for science and technology, the Alexander Graham Bell Award presented by the Alexander Graham Bell Association for the Deaf, the A.M. Turing Award from the ACM, the Silver Medal of the International Telecommunications Union, and the IEEE Alexander Graham Bell Medal, among many others. He holds a Ph.D. in computer science from the University of California, Los Angeles (UCLA), and more than a dozen honorary degrees.

ROBERT P. "BOB" COLWELL is an electrical engineer who worked at Intel and was director of the Microsystems Technology Office (MTO) at DARPA. He was the chief IA-32 architect on the Pentium Pro, Pentium II, Pentium III, and Pentium 4 microprocessors. Dr. Colwell retired from Intel in 2000. He was an Intel fellow from 1995 to 2000. He attended the University of Pittsburgh and gained an undergraduate degree in electrical engineering. He later attended CMU to get a Ph.D., also in electrical engineering. Dr. Colwell worked at a company called Multiflow in the late 1980s as a design engineer. In 1990, he joined Intel as a senior architect and was involved in the development of the P6 "core." The P6 core was used in the Pentium Pro, Pentium II, and Pentium III microprocessors, and designs derived from it are used in the Pentium M, Core Duo, and Core Solo, and Core 2 microprocessors sold by Intel. Dr. Colwell earned the ACM Eckert-Mauchly Award in 2005 and wrote the "At Random" column for *Computer,* a journal published by the IEEE Computer Society. He is as well the author of several papers in addition to *The Pentium Chronicles: The People, Passion, and Politics Behind Intel's Landmark Chips.* Dr. Colwell has spoken at universities on the challenges in chip design and management principles needed to tackle them.

DAVID CULLER is a professor of electrical engineering and computer sciences (EECS) at the University of California, Berkeley. He received his B.A. from UC Berkeley in 1980 and his M.S. and Ph.D. degrees from MIT in 1985 and 1989, respectively. He joined the EECS faculty in 1989 and is the founding director of Intel Research, UC Berkeley, and was associate chair of the EECS department, 2010-2012, and chair from 2012 through June 30, 2014. He won the Okawa Prize in 2013. He is a member of the NAE, an ACM fellow, and an IEEE fellow. He has been named one of *Scientific American*'s Top 50 Researchers and the creator of one of MIT's *Technology Review*'s 10 Technologies That Will Change th World. He was awarded the National Science Foundation (NSF) Presidential Young Investigator and the Presidential Faculty Fellowship. His research addresses networks of small, embedded wireless devices, planetary-scale Internet services, parallel computer architecture, parallel programming languages, and high-performance communication. It includes TinyOS, Berkeley Motes, PlanetLab, Networks of Workstations (NOW), Internet services, Active Messages, Split-C, and the Threaded Abstract Machine (TAM).

DEBORAH ESTRIN is a professor of computer science at Cornell Tech in New York City and a professor of public health at Weill Cornell Medical College. She is founder of the Healthier Lift Hub and directs the Small Data Lab at Cornell Tech. Dr. Estrin is also co-founder of the nonprofit startup Open mHealth. Her current focus is on mobile health and small data, leveraging the pervasiveness of mobile devices and digital interactions for health and life management. Previously, Dr. Estrin was on the UCLA faculty, where she was the founding director of the NSF Center for Embedded Networked Sensing (CENS), pioneering the development of mobile and wireless systems to collect and analyze real-time data about the physical world. Her honors include the ACM Athena Lecture (2006) and the Anita Borg Institute's Women of Vision Award for Innovation (2007). She is a member of the American Academy of Arts and Sciences and the NAE.

ANDREA GOLDSMITH is the Stephen Harris Professor in the School of Engineering and a professor of electrical engineering at Stanford University. She was previously on the faculty of Electrical Engineering at Caltech. She co-founded and serves as chief scientist of Accelera, Inc., which develops software-defined wireless network technology, and previously co-founded and served as CTO of Quantenna Communications, Inc., which develops high-performance Wi-Fi chipsets. She previously held positions at Maxim Technologies, Memorylink Corporation, and AT&T Bell Laboratories. Dr. Goldsmith is a fellow of the IEEE and of Stanford University, and she has received several awards for her work, including the IEEE Communications Society and Information Theory Society joint paper award, the IEEE Communications Society Best Tutorial Paper Award, the NAE Gilbreth Lecture Award, the IEEE ComSoc Communications Theory Technical Achievement Award, the IEEE ComSoc

Wireless Communications Technical Achievement Award, the Alfred P. Sloan Fellowship, and the *Silicon Valley/San Jose Business Journal*'s Women of Influence Award. She is author of the book *Wireless Communications* and coauthor of the books *MIMO Wireless Communications and Principles of Cognitive Radio,* all published by Cambridge University Press. Her research includes work on wireless information and communication theory, cognitive radios, sensor networks, "green" wireless system design, control systems closed over wireless networks, smart grid sensing and control, and applications of communications and signal processing to biology and neuroscience. She received B.S., M.S., and Ph.D. degrees in electrical engineering from UC Berkeley. Dr. Goldsmith is currently on the steering committee for the *IEEE Transactions on Wireless Communications* and previously served as editor for the *IEEE Transactions on Information Theory,* the *Journal on Foundations and Trends in Communications and Information Theory and in Networks, IEEE Transactions on Communications*, and *IEEE Wireless Communications.* Dr. Goldsmith participates actively in committees and conference organization for the IEEE Information Theory and Communications Societies and has served on the board of governors for both societies. She has been a distinguished lecturer for both societies, served as the president of the IEEE Information Theory Society in 2009, founded and chaired the student committee of the IEEE Information Theory Society, and currently chairs the Emerging Technology Committee and is a member of the Strategic Planning Committee in the IEEE Communications Society. At Stanford, she received the inaugural University Postdoc Mentoring Award and has been active in committees to innovate and revise both graduate and undergraduate education university-wide. She served as chair of Stanford's faculty senate in 2009 and currently serves on its faculty senate and on its budget group.

ERIC HORVITZ is a distinguished scientist at Microsoft Research. His interests span theoretical and practical challenges with developing systems that perceive, learn, and reason. His contributions include advances in principles and applications of machine learning and inference, search and retrieval, human–computer interaction, bioinformatics, and e-commerce. He has been elected a fellow of the AAAI and of the AAAS. He currently serves on the NSF Computer and Information Science and Engineering (CISE) advisory board and on the council of the Computing Community Consortium. He received his Ph.D. and M.D. degrees at Stanford University.

FARNAM JAHANIAN serves as vice president for research at CMU. He brings to CMU extensive leadership and administrative expertise, not only in supporting and nurturing research within and across disciplines, but also in translating research into innovative tools and technologies that succeed in the marketplace. The Office of the Vice President for Research at CMU is responsible for nurturing excellence in research, scholarship, and creative activities across the entire campus. It has overall responsibility for research administration and policy, provides oversight for responsible conduct of research and compliance, and focuses on facilitating and accelerating the movement of research and technology from the university to the marketplace. The Office of Sponsored Programs, Office of Research Integrity and Compliance, Center for Technology Transfer, and Office of Government Relations, and the Software Engineering Institute, among others, report to the vice president for research. Before CMU, Dr. Jahanian led the NSF Directorate for CISE from 2011 to 2014. He was on the faculty at the University of Michigan from 1993 to 2014, where he held the Edward S. Davidson Collegiate Professorship in the College of Engineering and served as chair for computer science and engineering from 2007 to 2011 and as director of the Software Systems Laboratory from 1997 to 2000. Previously, he held research and management positions at the IBM T.J. Watson Research Center. While at the University of Michigan, Dr. Jahanian led several large-scale research projects that studied the growth and scalability of the Internet infrastructure, which ultimately transformed how cyberthreats are addressed by Internet Service Providers. His research on Internet infrastructure security formed the basis for the successful Internet security services company Arbor Networks, which he co-founded in 2001. Dr. Jahanian served as chairman of Arbor Networks until its acquisition in 2010. He has been an active advocate for how basic research can be uniquely central to an innovation ecosystem that drives global competitiveness and addresses national priorities. He received numerous awards for his innovative research, commitment to education, and technology commercialization activities. He was named Distinguished University Innovator at the University of Michigan in 2009 and received the Governor's University Award for Commercialization Excellence in 2005. Dr. Jahanian holds a master's degree and a Ph.D. in computer science from the University of Texas, Austin. He is a fellow of the ACM, IEEE, and the AAAS.

MARGARET MARTONOSI is the Hugh Trumbull Adams '35 Professor of Computer Science at Princeton University, where she has been on the faculty since 1994. She also holds an affiliated faculty appointment in Princeton's Department of Electrical Engineering. From 2005 to 2007, she served as associate dean for academic affairs for the Princeton University School of Engineering and Applied Science. In 2011, she served as acting director of Princeton's Center for Information Technology Policy. Dr. Martonosi's research interests are in computer architecture and mobile computing, with particular focus on power-efficient systems. Her work has included the development of the Wattch power modeling tool and the Princeton ZebraNet mobile sensor network project for the design and real-world deployment of zebra tracking collars in Kenya. Her current research focuses on hardware–software interface approaches to manage heterogeneous parallelism and power-performance trade-offs in systems ranging from smartphones to chip multiprocessors to large-scale data centers. Dr. Martonosi is a fellow of both the IEEE and the ACM. She was the 2013 recipient of the Anita Borg Institute Technical Leadership Award. She has also received the 2013 NCWIT Undergraduate Research Mentoring Award and the 2010 Princeton University Graduate Mentoring Award. In addition to having authored many archival publications, Dr. Martonosi is an inventor on six granted U.S. patents and has coauthored a technical reference book on power-aware computer architecture. She serves on the board of directors of the Computing Research Association. Dr. Martonosi completed her Ph.D. at Stanford University and also holds a master's degree from Stanford and a bachelor's degree from Cornell University, all in electrical engineering.

STEFAN SAVAGE is a professor at the Department of Computer Science and Engineering at University of California, San Diego (UCSD). Dr. Savage's research interests lie at the intersection of distributed systems, networking, and computer security, with a current focus on embedded security and the economics of cybercrime. He currently serves as director of UCSD's Center for Network Systems and as co-director for the Cooperative Center for Internet Epidemiology and Defenses, a joint effort between UCSD and the International Computer Science Institute. Dr. Savage received his Ph.D. in computer science and engineering from the University of Washington and a bachelor's in applied history from CMU.

THAD STARNER is a wearable computing pioneer. He is a professor in the School of Interactive Computing at the Georgia Institute of Technology and a technical lead on Google Glass. He has been wearing a computer with a head-up display as part of his daily life since 1993, perhaps the longest such experience known. Besides Glass, his projects include a wireless glove that teaches how to play piano melodies without active attention by the wearer; a game for deaf children using sign language recognition that helps them acquire language skills; creating wearable computers to enable two-way communication experiments with wild dolphins; making wearable computers for working dogs to better communicate with their handlers; recovering phrase-level sign language from brain signals; and recognizing speech without vocalizing. Dr. Starner is a founder of the annual ACM/IEEE International Symposium on Wearable Computers, now in its 18th year, and has produced more than 400 papers and presentations on his work. He is an inventor on more than 60 U.S. patents awarded or in process.

DUNCAN WATTS is a principal researcher at Microsoft Research and a founding member of the MSR New York City laboratory. He is also an A.D. White Professor at Large at Cornell University as well as a visiting fellow at Columbia University and at Nuffield College, Oxford. Before joining MSR in 2012, he was, from 2000 to 2007, a professor of sociology at Columbia University and then a principal research scientist at Yahoo! Research, where he directed the Human Social Dynamics group. His research on social networks and collective dynamics has appeared in a wide range of journals, including *Nature, Science, Physical Review Letters,* the *American Journal of Sociology,* and *Harvard Business Review.* He has been recognized by the 2009 German Physical Society Young Scientist Award for Socio and Econophysics, the 2013 Lagrange-CRT Foundation Prize for Complexity Science, and the 2014 Everett Rogers Prize. He is the author of three books: *Six Degrees: The Science of a Connected Age, Small Worlds: The Dynamics of Networks between Order and Randomness,* and *Everything Is Obvious: Once You Know the Answer.* He holds a B.Sc. in physics from the Australian Defence Force Academy, from which he also received his officer's commission in the Royal Australian Navy, and a Ph.D. in theoretical and applied mechanics from Cornell University.

The National Academies of
SCIENCES · ENGINEERING · MEDICINE

The **National Academy of Sciences** was established in 1863 by an Act of Congress, signed by President Lincoln, as a private, nongovernmental institution to advise the nation on issues related to science and technology. Members are elected by their peers for outstanding contributions to research. Dr. Ralph J. Cicerone is president.

The **National Academy of Engineering** was established in 1964 under the charter of the National Academy of Sciences to bring the practices of engineering to advising the nation. Members are elected by their peers for extraordinary contributions to engineering. Dr. C. D. Mote, Jr., is president.

The **National Academy of Medicine** (formerly the Institute of Medicine) was established in 1970 under the charter of the National Academy of Sciences to advise the nation on medical and health issues. Members are elected by their peers for distinguished contributions to medicine and health. Dr. Victor J. Dzau is president.

The three Academies work together as the **National Academies of Sciences, Engineering, and Medicine** to provide independent, objective analysis and advice to the nation and conduct other activities to solve complex problems and inform public policy decisions. The Academies also encourage education and research, recognize outstanding contributions to knowledge, and increase public understanding in matters of science, engineering, and medicine.

Learn more about the National Academies of Sciences, Engineering, and Medicine at **www.national-academies.org**.

Other Recent Reports of the Computer Science and Telecommunications Board

Telecommunications Research and Engineering at the Institute for Telecommunication Sciences of the Department of Commerce: Meeting the Nation's Telecommunications Needs (2015)

Telecommunications Research and Engineering at the Communications Technology Laboratory of the Department of Commerce: Meeting the Nation's Telecommunications Needs (2015)

A Review of the Next Generation Air Transportation System: Implications and Importance of System Architecture (2015)

Bulk Collection of Signals Intelligence: Technical Options (2015)

Future Directions for NSF Advanced Computing Infrastructure to Support U.S. Science and Engineering in 2017-2020: An Interim Report (2014)

At the Nexus of Cybersecurity and Public Policy: Some Basic Concepts and Issues (2014)

Geotargeted Alerts and Warnings: Report of a Workshop on Current Knowledge and Research Gaps (2013)

Professionalizing the Nation's Cybersecurity Workforce? Criteria for Future Decision-Making (2013)

Public Response to Alerts and Warnings Using Social Media: Summary of a Workshop on Current Knowledge and Research Gaps (2013)

Continuing Innovation in Information Technology (2012)

Computing Research for Sustainability (2012)

The Future of Computing Performance: Game Over or Next Level? (2011)

Wireless Technology Prospects and Policy Options (2011)

Limited copies of CSTB reports are available free of charge from

Computer Science and Telecommunications Board
National Academies of Sciences, Engineering, and Medicine
Keck Center of the National Academies
500 Fifth Street, NW, Washington, DC 20001
(202) 334-2605/cstb@nas.edu
www.cstb.org